Lasting Love

What Keeps Couples Together

Judy C. Pearson

For Howard and Pat,
Happy Days!
Christmas 1995
Judy C. Pearson

 WCB   Wm. C. Brown Publishers

Contents

Acknowledgements

Many people talked to me about my topic during the writing of this book. I cannot credit each of them by name, but I appreciate all of the thoughtful and interesting comments people provided. I spoke with people whose marriages were as new as eight months and one couple who had been married as long as seventy-one years. A widow whose husband had died twenty years earlier told me that she was as in love with him today as she had been during their fifty years of marriage. To all of you, thank you for sharing your stories of marital happiness with me.

I want to single out people I have come to call "my couples." One of the husbands in the study referred to his wife as "my Cookie." In the same way, I began to refer to these loving women and men possessively. They gave me a minimum of 1 1/2 hours and sometimes as much as five hours sharing their experiences. Some have called with additional information, and a few have written me letters expressing thoughts they had not previously shared. In order to protect their disclosures, pseudonyms have been assigned to each couple. These pseudonyms have been consistently used so that the reader can follow the strands of individual stories throughout *Lasting Love*. I have attempted to use names of similar ethnic origin in order that the reader might draw conclusions about the similarity or diversity of families of distinctive ethnic backgrounds. I thank each of my couples by their actual names here:

Henry & Mildred Allen
Sally & Gene Beare
Suzanne & Earl Behning
John & Bonnie Binnick
Ilse & Chris Blunt
JoElle & Bud Boyers
Frances & Augusta Brady
Margaret & Marty Brennan
Lucille & Paul Cherchia
Virginia & Jones Dickinson
Marie & Jack Doyle
Bill & Marietta Ekberg
Blair & Dorothy Garland
Neal & Coleen Hawley
Jane & Larry Hitler
Jim & Helen Hoolihan
Wendell & Marjorie Jones
Muriel & Bert LaCrosse
Don & Nellie Long
Rayford & Doris McCreary
Sally & George Maloomian
Don & Dorothy Manecke
Paul & Mary Anna Morton
Dot & Al Parker
Don & Charlotte Pernik
Katherine & Claire Peterson
Virginia & Russell Reddig
Ute & Bill Reid
Donna & Don Rustad
Shirley & Dan Sullivan
August & Lois Summer
Robert & Alice Walker
Nick & Joyce Weisner
Edmund & Pauline Wojtowicz

A number of people read earlier versions of my manuscript, and I wish to acknowledge Belva Andrews, Michael J. Bugeja, Leda Cooks, Sue DeWine, Paul E. Nelson, Eve B. Shelnutt, Richard West, and Patricia Westfall. Their comments improved the manuscript in significant ways.

An Introduction

"What is REAL?" asked the Rabbit one day, when they were lying side by side near the nursery fender, before Nana came to tidy the room. "Does it mean having things that buzz inside you and a stick-out handle?"

"Real isn't how you are made," said the Skin Horse. "It's a thing that happens to you. When a child loves you for a long, long time, not just to play with, but REALLY loves you, then you become Real."

"Does it hurt?" asked the Rabbit.

"Sometimes," said the Skin Horse, for he was always truthful. "When you are Real you don't mind being hurt."

"Does it happen all at once, like being wound up," he asked, "or bit by bit?"

"It doesn't happen all at once," said the Skin Horse. "You become. It takes a long time. That's why it doesn't often happen to people who break easily, or have sharp edges, or who have to be carefully kept. Generally, by the time you are Real, most of your hair has been loved off, and your eyes drop out and you get loose in the joints and very shabby. But these things don't matter at all, because once you are Real you can't be ugly, except to people who don't understand."

—Margery Williams, *The Velveteen Rabbit*

Chapter 1

Marriage for a Lifetime: Illusion or Reality?

The greatest happiness and the deepest satisfaction in life, the most intense enthusiasm and the most profound inner peace, all come from being a member of a loving family.

—Sven Wahlroos, *Family Communication*

In Madame Toussaud's Wax Museum in London, visitors are encouraged to pose with lifelike replicas of contemporary figures, such as, J. R. Ewing, the Beatles, and Alfred Hitchcock. The first thought you have upon meeting Kenneth Harris, Jr., is that you have been transported to Madame Toussaud's. Kenneth Harris, Jr., is of medium height, a slight build, and he wears a hearing aid. But you do not see these normal features at first. Your eye is drawn instead to the yellow, smooth skin which is identical to the sculpting wax used to duplicate a living person. The bushy white eyebrows do nothing to dissuade you. You can almost see the pricks in the wax where the artist's needle inserted the human hairs. His choice of clothing—a matching pale blue shirt, sweater, and socks with coordinating blue plaid sports pants—only adds to the illusion. Kenneth Harris, Jr., is ninety years old, and despite his appearance, he is a flesh-and-blood human being.

Jane Harris is ninety-three, but she looks very real. Her skin is as wrinkled as her husband's is not. She has small blue eyes and large white teeth. While Kenneth has chosen a sporty outfit, she is dressed more formally. She is adorned in a light blue sheer blouse, a blue hand-knitted sweater, a straight blue skirt, matching low-heeled blue shoes, and a pale shade of grey hose. Gold and blue earrings complete the outfit. Jane is a lady waiting to welcome guests for tea.

The Harrises' home resembles Jane rather than Kenneth in its formal appointments. While the Harris couple has chosen a fifth-floor condominium overlooking the Gulf of Mexico in which to spend their remaining years, the space has been transformed into an elegant single-family dwelling. The Harrises' home is filled with beautiful paintings and antiques. Every dish, every piece of silver, every piece of beautiful furniture, is steeped in tradition and elegance. Recorded piano music plays in the background. The recording is of Jane, who was an accomplished concert pianist years before.

Kenneth and Jane Harris have celebrated seventy-one years of marriage.

• • •

Why do the marriages of people in their sixties and seventies keep on ticking while those of people in their forties and younger take a licking? One answer is simple timing. People married fifty years ago married for life, and—regardless of circumstances—they remained married. People who were married in the 1930s and 1940s believed that their marriage was for life. Usually, it was.

People in such marriages know how to have happy marriages as well as long ones. What do they know and what can we learn from them? This book will reveal information that will surprise and tantalize. The people are as real as their stories, and their ideas are timely for the couple seeking lasting love in the 1990s and into the twenty-first century.

• • •

Just after the turn of the century, a little boy was born to Kenneth Harris, Sr., a professor of Romance languages at the University of Pennsylvania, and his wife, Alice. Before the child was born, the couple agreed that if their firstborn was male, Kenneth would determine the nature of his education. Ken Jr., called Kenny by the family, and his brilliant father found each other to be family comrades for life.

When Kenny was three years old, his education began. His father and two colleagues from the university instructed the little boy in a program that lasted ten hours every day, six days a week, 365 days a year. Sunday was the only day he did not receive instruction. He did not play with other children, and he never attended formal school.

Kenny's father knew he was experimenting with his son's education, but he had no malicious intentions. He never touched his son, except in an affectionate way. He never criticized the boy in his entire life.

Kenny's mother, who had agreed with the arrangement during gestation, became resentful. The couple had two more children, and before they were born, she convinced her husband that she would be in charge of them. She acquiesced 100 percent on Kenny's rearing since she was allowed to manage the affairs of the two younger daughters.

When Kenny was thirteen, his father died unexpectedly. As a college professor, he had little money saved or invested. Kenny's mother was destitute and had a family of four for whom to provide. Responding as did many widowed women of the time, she quickly remarried. Her second husband was not as sensitive nor as kind as her first, and a particular antipathy developed between this rough-hewn man and her first husband's namesake.

Kenny was not only struggling with an antagonistic relationship with a new stepfather; without his tutors, he was required to attend public school. He completed high school in one term and graduated with honors, but he was very unhappy. At the age of fourteen, as a high school graduate, he saw no reason to stay in a home in which anger and conflict dominated. Kenny's mother argued constantly with her new husband, but she had no economic independence. Kenny felt that she was doomed to an unhappy conclusion to her life and that his little sisters, who were still in grammar school, could similarly not escape the conflict-habituated home. Kenny felt that he was the only one who could escape this house of hostility.

In 1916, the United States military was eager for new recruits. Kenny, who became known thereafter as Kenneth, had no trouble convincing the naval recruiting officers that he was eighteen years old, although he was barely fourteen. The navy was simply looking for warm bodies, and the chief boatswain's mate who interviewed him asked few questions. Kenneth thus joined the navy and fought in the First World War as a teenager.

• • •

People have probably always wanted long and satisfying relationships. In *Modern Man in Search of a Soul*, Carl Jung wrote, "About a third of my cases are suffering from no clinically definable neurosis, but from the senselessness and emptiness of their lives. This can be described as the general neurosis of our times." In his book *When All You've Ever Wanted Isn't Enough: The Search for a Life that Matters,* Harold Kushner adds,

> A leading anthropologist who had spent years studying chimpanzees in the wild once wrote, "One chimpanzee is no chimpanzee." That is, a chimpanzee can develop into a real chimpanzee only in the company of other chimps. Isolated in a zoo, it may survive but will never become its real self. I have been observing people in their natural habitat for at least as long as Dr. Leakey studied chimps, and I would paraphrase his comment to read, "One human being is no human being." None of us can be truly human in isolation. The qualities that make us human emerge only in the ways we relate to other people.

Today couples express even greater interest in commitment than they have in recent years. Why? Some experts suggest that the presence of AIDS, in particular, has encouraged fewer partners and therefore more lasting relationships. Psychologist Catherine Johnson in *New Woman* magazine disagrees with these experts. "The real change isn't due to medical phenomena, it's emotional. . . . Men and women want to connect. . . . People want to be faithful again." She projects, "What we could be witnessing is the effect of market economics: as love and marriage become more scarce, they become accordingly more valuable. . . . And because having a good marriage is a paramount goal, mutual fidelity is once again a priority. . . . Today, people wish and hope to be faithful to their partner."

Baby Boomers are the CEOs of today's emotional and social corporations. And Baby Boomers care more about relationships. Demographer Cheryl Russell, in *100 Predictions for the Baby Boom,* reports that more than nine out of ten Baby Boom men and women say that marriage is the best possible life-style. Whatever Baby Boomers want, the culture gets. As the Baby Boomers hit their thirties and forties, "thirtysomething" and cocooning become the rage.

Catherine Johnson points to the new popularity of cocooning. "Baby Boomers who once spent their evenings making the scene now opt to hole up together in front of the VCR, forming cozy, tight-knit little cocoons. . . . Cocooning is to the eighties what togetherness was to the fifties. . . . The rat race encourages cocooning. . . . When people are desperately in need of some peace and quiet, monogamy is a better choice than infidelity . . . probably sometime in your 30s—it is fidelity, commitment, and responsibility that make you bigger and better . . . after a point, constant partner swapping probably *is* a personal failure.'' She concludes, ''In the final analysis, the reason the new fidelity is upon us is . . . because for a huge proportion of the population the time is right.'' Indeed, for some, the time is now.

• • •

Toward the end of the First World War, Kenneth Harris was stationed in the navy yard in Brooklyn, New York. His father's college roommate had a daughter just older than he. One Saturday afternoon, with little else to do, he phoned Barbara. He invited her to visit him on the 110-foot submarine chaser on which he lived. Barbara asked if she should bring her friend Jane, who was at her home. Kenneth agreed, not knowing that he was about to meet his future wife.

Jane Smith was thrilled to be invited to the naval vessel. She pictured a huge ship with officers in white uniforms and gloves. She dressed accordingly, wearing a long, tight white skirt. She was dismayed to find the submarine chaser and was embarrassed that she had to lift her skirt above her ankles to clear the wash rails at the edge of the boat. In the early twentieth century, a lady did not expose her ankles to a gentleman. When she later revealed her indiscretion, her mother was mortified by her daughter's lewd behavior. Jane thought her mother to be prudish.

Jane did not ask Kenneth his age, but she noticed his discharge papers, which he had just received signaling his upcoming discharge, during this first meeting. The discharge papers listed Kenneth's current age as twenty-two, which was based on his original enlistment age of eighteen. In fact, Kenneth was just eighteen, since he had started his tour of duty at the age of fourteen.

Kenneth fell in love at first sight, but Jane did not. She had a crush on the minister in her church. The minister was fourteen years older than she and did nothing to encourage her. In fact, he counseled her that she would not have a satisfying life as the wife of a minister. Although Jane gradually came to accept her pastor's advice, she continued to look for an older man.

After Jane had met Kenneth she told her friend Barbara that he seemed immature, even though he was a year older than she. She said she preferred much older men and was determined to find someone at least a decade older than she and probably with a profession already established.

5

Kenneth was even more determined than Jane. He knew what he wanted, and he began to court Jane in earnest. He used persuasion, personal appeals, arguments, and persistence. Jane began to observe that Kenneth was intelligent and very handsome; nonetheless, she was wary. She noted to Barbara, "He's very determined."

When Kenneth gave Jane his mother's engagement ring from his father, she was very impressed and agreed to marry him. A few months later, she backed out and returned the ring. Her older sister's marriage had ended in a disaster, and she did not want to make the same mistake.

Kenneth remained steadfast and continued to woo his reluctant bride. She accepted the ring once more, and the two were married soon thereafter. She confided in her sister, "I love him undoubtedly, but not unquestioningly."

Kenneth knew that Jane wanted to marry a man much older than she and resisted revealing his actual age until the two were safely married. If the beginning of their marriage was shaky, this information did nothing to help matters; however, Jane and Kenneth were later to report that their union of seventy-plus years was truly satisfying—one of the happiest of all those they knew.

• • •

How do people maintain satisfying relationships? How can an individual predict a happy or doomed marriage? Scientist Niels Bohr wrote, tongue-in-cheek, "Prediction is difficult, especially about the future." Can anyone provide help for those engaged in meeting and mating?

More basic, what is a happy marriage? Happiness, researchers say, is not the absence of sadness, but a distinct emotion in marriage. It is not measured by experts but by the partners themselves. If you want to know "who's naughty and who's nice," you don't ask marriage counselors, you ask marital partners.

Because the players are the ones to know, satisfying marriages come in more flavors than Baskin-Robbins ice cream. Wide variations exist. One couple needs a lot of sexual contact, while another prefers little or none. People's backgrounds, their observations of others, their developmental period, and their own experiences alter their perceptions of the happy marriage. Individual diversity translates into individual happiness.

Marital happiness, or satisfaction, is not the same as marital stability. Marital stability is the endurance or likelihood of endurance of a marriage. Marriages can be long lasting, but not necessarily satisfying to the couple. Bad marriages can be neither long lasting nor satisfying. Some marriages may be satisfying but not stable. A marital couple, physically separated by their individual professions, may terminate their relationship even though they care deeply for each other and have had a satisfying relational life. Finally, marriage can be both stable and satisfying, which is the ideal toward which most of us strive and which is the focus of this book.

Marital satisfaction is more than luck or an "idiot lottery." Communication plays a vital role. This book explores the relationship between happy marriages and communication. J. K. Alberts, at California State, Los Angeles, notes, "In romantic relationships talk must accomplish many purposes—signal interest, declare love, join couples in marriage. However, it must also function in other, less pleasant ways, such as arguing and complaining. Using talk to express negative emotions and dissatisfaction can be uncomfortable and/or unsuccessful for many couples." Communication includes how we fight and how we make up, how we seduce and love each other, and how we handle our daily need for help, touch, tenderness, and affection. The words of couples married a minimum of forty years provide poignant examples.

What is communication? Everyone from the person on the street to the most recently heralded expert on Oprah attests to the importance of communication in personal relationships. Most people simply mean "talk" when they use the word. Or, they are referring to the importance of sharing your feelings. Popular platitudes encouraging talking and "sharing all" ought to be accompanied by a warning that this behavior may be hazardous to your psychological and relational health.

We can define communication more precisely and more usefully. Communication is the process whereby people creatively interpret verbal and nonverbal cues to establish shared meanings with others. Understanding and sharing are basic to the communicative process. We gain meaning when we socially interact with others. That meaning continually changes and shifts as we respond to interactions and as our understanding of it changes.

Communication, defined this way, is vital to a satisfying family life. According to communication expert Art Bochner, "The most fundamental aspect of family process is communication." Understanding marital communication is important because it is largely through interaction that marriages are satisfying or dissatisfying.

Leslie Baxter, who teaches at the University of California in Davis, and Kathryn Dindia, from the University of Wisconsin–Milwaukee, explain, "Relationships are dynamic social processes in which the parties must engage in ongoing 'relationship work' if their bond is to remain viable." An understanding of the role of communication in marriages will enhance the likelihood of relational happiness. Indeed, an understanding of the communicative process may be the most important factor in achieving a long and happy marriage.

• • •

Although Kenneth and Jane Harris have had a long and satisfying marriage that has lasted over seventy years, a great deal of distress and troubles have interceded. Kenneth's mental breakdowns, Jane's ill health, and the burden of being without college educations plagued them as they moved from home to home in the northeastern part of the country, finally settling in Florida after they had been married fifty years.

Kenneth Harris had an unusual childhood. He did not attend school until he was fourteen, tutored instead by his father and his father's colleagues from the University of Pennsylvania. His atypical childhood may have been at least partly responsible for the mental breakdowns he suffered throughout his adult years. Before he retired, he had experienced five such breakdowns, resulting in hospitalization and behavioral modification.

The first time he experienced a breakdown, Jane did not understand that anything was wrong. She told a friend at the time, "Kenneth has turned on his family." After the initial illness, she began to understand her husband's disease and also learned that for his own protection he had to be in a sanatorium. She explained to her own parents, "He will physically wreck himself, but it is very, very difficult to commit him."

Kenneth placed great pressure on himself. He learned that pressure is the cause for many manic-depressive conditions. He admitted after one such breakdown, "The individual doesn't have to put this stress on himself, and he may complain, if he's silly enough, that others are doing it to me. Well, you can't let others do it for you unless you're willing to do it yourself. That's just it."

Most of Kenneth's breakdowns began with a lack of sleep. He told one of his psychiatrists, "I can't shut down or turn off my mind. I have never learned how to shut off my mind, and shut it down completely. I can't sleep. My mind is physically breaking down. I'm damaging it." He added, "I go to bed and I develop feverish conditions. I feel myself turning red, heating up after two or three days without sleep."

Kenneth learned that the only way he could become healthy was to be committed to a sanatorium and to be shut off from the rest of the world. He viewed it as a "country club life." Kenneth stayed in the hospital for a couple of months each of the first four times he was committed, but recurrences convinced his doctor to insist on a longer stay the fifth time he was committed. Until the physician was convinced that Kenneth understood the nature of his illness, he refused to release him. Apparently, the doctor knew best; Kenneth has not suffered another depression nor has he been hospitalized for mental problems since.

In 1953, after being in the sanatorium for eleven months, Kenneth stepped out of the motion picture business in which he had developed a successful, although brief, career. Just before he left the hospital, Dr. Hamilton, his physician, told him, "Kenneth, you've got enough money to live for the rest of your life. You don't need any more money. So why are you doing this to yourself?"

Kenneth responded quickly, "I work because I love it."

Dr. Hamilton was firm. "Look what it's done to you. I don't care how much you want to create new things. You've got to get out of the business."

Although he was only fifty-one years old, he took his doctor's orders seriously.

Jane's health also caused strain on the marriage, which has spanned over seven decades. She developed pericarditis, induced by a pleurisy. An inflammation of the pericardium itself squeezes the heart and crushes it to the point where damage is just the same as if you've had a massive coronary. Her physician insisted that the couple move from the northern part of the country to the South. He told Kenneth, "You must get her out of this climate at any cost. Don't ever spend another winter up here. You must make some arrangements to go somewhere. I don't care if you go to Florida, California, or Arizona, but go there and make sure she spends her winters there. Because if she gets that pleurisy, she'll die, and nothing will save her."

The couple moved to South Florida, but Jane felt the loss of her lifetime friends. Then a second blow was struck. Although Jane had been a concert pianist, she developed severe arthritis in her hands, and surgery became necessary. After the operation, her fingers no longer had the flexibility needed to play the piano. Jane was now without her friends and her lifetime avocation.

A woman in her early nineties, Jane has a bad heart and she tires easily. Kenneth concludes, "She lives on nitroglycerin."

Jane admits, "I also have cataracts. I have a lot of things, little things, you know, that all old-aged people have. But as long as I can walk and dress myself, and we do all our own work here, I am all right."

Although both Kenneth and Jane are highly gifted individuals, neither received a college education. Jane particularly has been embarrassed about this deficit. Her husband's family, her own children, and most of their friends are highly educated people.

Jane and Kenneth's two children, both boys, are doctors. Both sons are in their sixties. Stan, the older son, is a professor of pediatrics at the University of Maryland as well as the chief of pediatrics at Mercy Hospital in Baltimore. Ben, the younger son, is a radiologist and has made well over ten thousand angiograms. His headquarters are in Richmond, Virginia, and he has also taught clinical radiology at the medical college of the University of Virginia. He went through the Cleveland Clinic and graduated from Case Western Reserve. Both boys, like their paternal grandfather, landed in the ivory tower. The granddaughters, too, teach in colleges and universities.

Kenneth reflected to a friend, "Five generations of my family have been in the ivory tower."

Jane sadly relates, "He never went to college. He was signed up for college when I met him. Instead, he married me."

Two decades ago, a woman queried Jane about Kenneth's education. Although the conversation occurred in 1970, Jane remembers it vividly. She recalls, "A very catty woman said to me, 'When are you going to celebrate your fiftieth anniversary?' We had already been married a little over fifty years. And so I said, 'We've already had it.' I told her, 'My husband was eighteen and I was twenty-one when we got married.' And she said, 'Oh but he never went to college, did he?' And she said it three times and the third time I said to her, 'You know, he worked with professors from M. I. T. and nobody questioned that; they were only interested in his knowledge.' She was determined to hurt me when she asked three times. It was clearly malicious."

What also is clear is how Jane and Kenneth appreciate each other's talents, sacrifices, and contributions, factors in a long and happy marriage.

• • •

Do the experts know what factors predict marital satisfaction? They know that some features don't make a difference. For example, a recent survey by the Consumers Union determined that age, education, religion, and health are not strong predictors of marital happiness. Similarly, where someone lived, whether they were a man or a woman, and their income do not predict satisfaction. However, the Consumers Union found that "wives and husbands who rate the quality of communications in their marriage as excellent or very good enjoy an astonishingly high proportion of happy marriages—the highest for any group in this study." They conclude, "We found that the wives and husbands most likely to be happily married after age 50 are those who maintain 'excellent' or 'very good' communications with their spouse."

Communication may provide one avenue to satisfying marriages. It has received strong recommendations. For example, professors Phillips and Goodall in their book *Loving and Living* write,

> Talk is the substance of a loving relationship. Talk enables
> lovers to exchange feelings and make agreements about
> their day-to-day life. In this way each couple develops their
> own unwritten constitutions, agreements about how decisions
> are to be made and carried out, how disputes are to be
> settled, how rituals and ceremonies will be conducted, and
> how they will deal with each other and everyone else.

Communication emerges in most research studies as essential to marital satisfaction. Classic studies by family researchers Lewis and Spanier identify communication as the major predictor of marital satisfaction. More recent work by Erich Kirchler, from the University of Linz, in Austria, suggests that happiness is associated with frequency, positivity, and effectiveness of spousal interaction.

Leo F. Buscaglia, best-selling author of *Living, Loving, and Learning* and *Loving Each Other: The Challenge of Human Relationships,* holds that to be happy, we need to feel needed. He notes, "If a relationship becomes destructive, endangers our human dignity, prevents us from growing, continually depresses and demoralizes us—and we have done everything we can to prevent its failure—then, unless we are masochists and enjoy misery, we must eventually terminate it." From his six hundred surveys, Buscaglia found that the basic ingredients to love were (1) communication, (2) honesty, (3) forgiveness, (4) joy, (5) ridding oneself of jealousy, and (6) intimacy. Communication emerged as the number one factor.

Family therapists and practitioners often recommend communication to troubled families. Sven Wahlroos, author of *Family*

Communication, is unequivocal, "In my two decades of practice as a clinical psychologist I have become convinced that the key to improvement of family relationships—and thereby to emotional health in general—lies in communication." Popular authors, too, recommend communication. Best-selling books such as Shere Hite's *Women and Love: A Cultural Revolution in Progress,* Warren Farrell's *Why Men Are the Way They Are,* and Deborah Tannen's *You Just Don't Understand: Women and Men in Conversation,* discuss the problems in maintaining satisfying relationships. These authors and others identify communication as an essential predictor of satisfaction.

Does everyone agree about the importance of communication in lasting relationships? Experts have given their opinions. College students who have never been married have been queried. Both satisfied and dissatisfied couples have filled out questionnaires explaining their level of satisfaction. However, one set of experts who have not been tapped are those in satisfying long-term marriages.

Older people in general may be a particularly good source of happiness. Dagmar O'Connor, trained by Masters and Johnson, wrote *How to Put the Love Back into Making Love.* Interviewed by Donna Jackson, senior editor of *New Woman,* she noted, "I did a study years ago where we found that younger women, who had many choices about what paths to take in life, had higher self-esteem than older women, who had fewer choices. But the older women rated themselves as being happier. So the impression I had after this study was that younger women have healthier self-esteem but they feel they have too many choices. They have more responsibility to choose and to choose correctly and so they feel less happy. Simply put, they worry more."

Consumers Union is one of the few groups that has realized the value of discussing love and sex with older people. It conducted a study of the sexual behaviors and attitudes of over four thousand people fifty years old and older. Most of these people had been married for thirty years or more and were in their first marriage; the rest were widowed, divorced, or never married. The findings do not support the stereotype that older people are sexually inactive, unhappy, or lonely. Although the Consumers Union asked respondents if they wanted to write about religion, transportation problems, and other concerns, their greatest interest was in writing about love and sexuality. "The vast majority were enthusiastic and candid in telling us and the world what their lives have been like since age 50."

Who can instruct individuals seeking satisfaction in their love relationship? In the last few years, researchers have begun to ask marital couples to discuss their relationship with them. Linda K. Acitelli, from the University of Connecticut, observes, "Only recently have marital researchers begun to explore spouses' perspectives of their own relationships." She adds, "The concept of relationship awareness has been introduced" . . . and it "is defined . . . as a person's thinking about interaction patterns, comparisons, or contrasts between himself or herself and the other partner in the relationship."

While Acitelli notes that few studies focus on relationship awareness, she encourages their use. In addition to learning about features of individuals' marriages, such research has an added benefit. Acitelli concludes, "Wives are . . . especially appreciative with regard to relationship talk if their husbands are speaking. Not only is it less expected and more exceptional for husbands to talk about relationships, the literature suggests that husbands' intimacy, maturity, and other interpersonal skills are correlated with couple satisfaction."

People who have satisfying marriages that span forty or fifty years may be able to reveal information that is useful to the young couple or the couple in mid-life who wish to someday mark a golden anniversary. All couples who married in the 1930s and 1940s are not happy. Indeed, people married for forty or fifty years may be together simply because traditional values allowed no other alternative. This book focuses only on those couples who perceive themselves, and whom others perceive, to be among the happiest of their acquaintances. They represent the crème de la crème of the satisfied couples. Not by prescription, but by telling their stories, these couples may provide models and examples that will be useful to others.

• • •

Kenneth and Jane Harris have had as many problems as any couple during their marriage, which has spanned seven decades. They also have known great joy and have had unique experiences on which to reflect. Their pain and problems have been offset by Kenneth's world-known inven-

13

tions, by friendships with people like Walt Disney, and by enormous wealth and success.

Kenneth did not attend college, but he was innately bright. During his middle years, after being given a commendation for his remarkable achievements, Kenneth remarked to a friend, "I'm an inventor, pure and simple. I'm a motion picture engineer." While his description may have been an accurate portrayal of his career, it was by far an understatement.

Kenneth describes the beginning of his career. "Walter Green was the president of the National Theatre Supply Company and the International Projector Corporation and also the executive vice-president. Now I'm going back to 1929. At that time, I was twenty-seven years old. He also was a very kindly individual who really treated me like a younger brother. Ten-and-a-half years older than I."

He picks up his career a few years later. "I'm one of the early members of the Society of Motion Picture Engineers. And I invented a motion picture screen very early in life, a time when sound came in. I invented the sound screen, which met a great deal of success around the world. I'd been fascinated by three-dimensional motion picture prospects for years before, and I'd made a great study of stereoscopic effects, and how they might be used. Because of my interest in stereoscopics, I happened to meet Jack Rule, who was a professor of graphics at M. I. T—a Harvard graduate—and who had done more work on stereoscopy than any other human being. Through him I met Edwin Land, from Polaroid, who became interested also for a short time in stereoscopy." Kenneth eventually invented the motion picture screen that was necessary for Walt Disney to produce Fantasia. Kenneth worked extensively with Disney and considered him to be a friend as well.

Kenneth grows philosophical. "I would never have been able to accomplish what I did had it not been for luck. I was born with a little golden angel, and it's been very kind to me. Luck is a very important issue. I had the best of good fortune. Time and time and time again. Over and over again in my life. I can't understand why, there isn't any rationale for it. But nevertheless, if being in the right place at the right time, with the right thought, with the right attitude, all this has to come together. And if it doesn't, you don't have it. But in addition to all that, that little sheer element of luck plays a great part."

• • •

Over two hundred couples volunteered to be part of this book. Why did they volunteer? A number of the couples explained that it was because the interview represented a "new experience" for them, and they like to try all kinds of new experiences. Some of them are simply helpful people. Interestingly, more men than women volunteered to be interviewed.

Of the couples who volunteered, forty were interviewed in depth. Thirty-four couples fit the requirements of having both satisfying and stable marriages that had lasted a minimum of forty years. Their words make up the bulk of this book.[1]

The stories these couples told surprised me, and they will, no doubt, surprise you. These are not elderly grandparents sitting quietly in their chairs reading tabloids and doing crossword puzzles. These are vital and active individuals who tell provocative, humorous, and optimistic stories as well as stories that are depressing, tortured, and astonishing. The couples reveal details of their life that they have heretofore told no one—including their spouse. They welcome you to *Lasting Love*. They open the door to the houses of their marriage and to the possibility of enhancing your chance for lasting love.

---

1. The actual names of the couples are not used in the text. Pseudonyms of similar ethnic origin are substituted to protect their privacy. The couples are all named and thanked in the preface.

Chapter 2

No Single Model: "We Never Talked Religion"

The most beautiful thing we can experience is the mysterious. It is the source of all true art and science.

—Albert Einstein

Duffy and Snookie Day are an offbeat twosome. They both walk tall, with Duffy at 6'6" towering over his wife who is 5'10". His most distinguishing characteristic is a steel wool crew cut. He dresses casually, in open-necked, short-sleeved button-front shirts. A small notebook in his breast pocket keeps important dates and telephone numbers close at hand. While conversing, he refers to the book from time to time.

Snookie is particularly tall for a woman who is over seventy. Yet she does not appear tall because her husband is much taller. She is well-proportioned with a medium build, but looks athletic rather than soft. She dresses in sporty outfits—often in blue and green. Her short hair is shot with gray. She is confident and calm.

Although the birthplaces of many couples married forty or more years ago were close to each other, Duffy and Snookie were born far apart—he in New York, she in Alabama. Snookie explains, "I came north looking for him and he came south looking for me. We met in Cincinnati at Proctor and Gamble." Duffy had gone to college at Yale, while Snookie had attended

Berea College in Kentucky. She had majored in sociology and psychology, and Duffy had majored in economics.

• • •

Many people theorize about what characterizes the marriage long and strong. Parents caution their children to marry someone of the same religion, educational level, or economic class. Others believe that a strong religious faith is important. The couples who demonstrated and reported satisfying, long-term marriages defied such prescriptions.

Consider the descriptive information about the thirty-four couples who were interviewed in-depth for this book. First, the marriages range from forty to seventy-one years in length; the average length of marriage is fifty years. The women's ages range from sixty-one to ninety-three years, and the average age is seventy-one years. A surprising number of women are youngest children (eleven), followed by those who are the oldest children (nine), only children (six), or middle children (two are second oldest, three are middle, and three are the second youngest children). The men's ages range from sixty-three to ninety years. with the average age being seventy-two years old. More of the men are the youngest children in their original families (twelve), followed by those who are the oldest (seven) or middle (six) children, second youngest (four) or only (four) children, followed by one man who is the second oldest child. Some of the couples do not have children. The range in number of children extends from none to nine. The average number of children per couple is three.

The couples in this book are representatives of such professions as medicine, dentistry, law, education, and business. Steelworkers and machinists are included, too. One two-star general officer spent two hours with me discussing his unique marriage. One man's grandparents were not married, and consequently his parents were born out of wedlock, because they were part of the Oneida community in New York. An inventor of games for the Milton Bradley Company and the man who invented the movie screen for stereophonic motion pictures are both in the group. One man's mother was Eleanor Roosevelt's close friend, and she was with Mrs. Roosevelt in the White House when Franklin Roosevelt died.

The group includes Protestants, Catholics, Jews, agnostics, and atheists. Thirty-seven are Protestant, twenty-seven are Catholic, three are atheist or agnostic, and one person is Jewish. Thirty-six individuals attend church or synagogue once a week, fourteen attend more than once a week, eight attend once a month, six attend less than once a year or never, and four attend once a year.

The educational level varies from those who did not complete high school to those with advanced or professional degrees. Thirty-two are high school graduates, twenty-six are college graduates, six hold advanced or professional degrees, and four did not complete high school. In fourteen of the marriages, the spouses have different educational levels—sometimes the husband has more education than his wife, and sometimes the wife has more education than her husband.

The couples are from New York, New Jersey, Massachusetts, Connecticut, Pennsylvania, Ohio, Michigan, Illinois, Indiana, Minnesota, North Dakota, Wisconsin, Alabama, Florida, Armenia, and Germany. The couples have moved, on the average, four times. After marrying, one couple stayed on homesteaded property with her parents; they have never moved away. A professional military couple has moved nearly forty times. Clearly, these couples do not fit a single pattern.

• • •

How did Duffy and Snookie Day meet? Both were employed by Proctor and Gamble in Cincinnati, Ohio. She was in the personnel department and had access to all of the files of the people working in the company. When she met Duffy, she was engaged to another man whom she had met in college. Everything was perfect in her relationship with John. His parents liked her, and she liked them; her parents liked him, and he liked them. However, because she was so busy, Snookie could never set a date for the wedding.

Then Duffy came along. He saw her first when she competed in athletic events for the company's annual picnic. Snookie won every event she entered and won a great deal of money, for the times. He confided in a friend, "That's the gal I'm going to marry." He fell in love at first sight.

How did Snookie feel about Duffy? He bothered her because, in her words, "I liked him too much. My life was happy; it was smooth. 'What is this thing coming into my life?' My old favorite expression is 'it was meant to be.' So finally he said to me one night, 'You've got to make your mind up.' And even John came to a party at Cincinnati, and he met Duffy and he said, 'You know, that guy is in love with you, and you think you're in love with him.' He knew it, too. It sounds very romantic, and it was, but something was working there. It was meant to be. I liked him too much."

• • •

Communication is important to the long, happy marriage, as experts have told us; however, it is not a simple matter of some easily learned communication skills. No single model of successful communication abilities emerged among the older happily married couples. Some people talk and some do not. Some have an outrageous sense of humor, and some are relatively humorless. Some bicker while others disdain disagreement.

This conclusion is not surprising if you are in a happy marriage and you know others who are very different from you but who seem similarly satisfied with their relationship. Happy couples vary in relative age, socioeconomic background, education, religion, and politics, as well as attitudes, values, and beliefs. People who are the youngest, oldest, and middle children in their original families can all claim to have happy marriages. Professional people as well as blue-collar workers may have ideal family lives. No religious group appears to have a hold on happiness, nor does regular attendance at church, mosque, or synagogue bear any necessary relationship to satisfaction. Some satisfied couples move frequently while others stay in one place. Some spend virtually every moment together, while others need time away from their mate.

What is important, as we shall determine again and again, is not the specific communication behaviors that happy couples enact. What is important is their interpretation of their interactions. Studies that suggest happiness in marriage is related to specific communication skills, such as confessing intimate details of life, listening in certain ways, and resolving conflict with specific resolution techniques, are suspect. What works wonders in one marriage may be an anathema in another.

One example of differences in communication behavior is in the relative power possessed by each member of the couple. Some happy marriages are egalitarian, while others are wife-dominated or husband-dominated. Marital partners behave in these ways over time, and the patterns they determine are oftentimes similar to those of their original families. If the couple's parents have equal relationships, then the couple may similarly have an egalitarian marriage. If their parent's marriages are traditionally male-dominated, the couple's marriage is more likely to mirror this kind of relationship.

Power is not quite so easily determined, however. Each member of the couple comes from a separate family, and these original, orienting families could display different power ratios. For example, the wife's family might be female-dominated, while the husband's family is male-dominated. A power struggle might ensue as the wife attempts to control the behaviors of the couple and as he similarly tries to be in charge.

The couple must thus negotiate the power relationship. Through communication, the two people create a shared reality. They negotiate a power relationship of their own. The pattern of power may be more similar to her parents, his parents, or neither set of parents. The power relationship could be very distinctive from either orienting family.

Researchers have shown that egalitarianism, generally valued in our culture, but not always practiced by married couples, is the pattern of choice for many marital partners. Marriages in which power is shared or split are most highly related to marital satisfaction. The second choice of couples is the husband-dominated pattern, and the distant third choice is the wife-dominated pattern. These preferences among couples may be based on their familiarity with them rather than on their actual choice.

Some of the long-term, happily married couples interviewed for this book have chosen an equal relationship. This equality has arisen from two different patterns. First, some couples discuss each issue and come to some agreement on it. A second set of couples divide the areas of responsibility for decision making. Diane and Herbert Norton, of Minneapolis, Minnesota, are egalitarian in both their interactions and their decision making. Both are Realtors. Diane recalls that Herbert was always in charge of choosing their automobiles, but Herbert remembers, "In charge, but not to the point where you didn't dare say anything. I bought a purple car one day and she didn't . . ."

Diane interrupts, "Oh, no, I didn't like purple!"

Herbert continues, "I bought a purple car, and she didn't particularly like it, so I had the top painted white, and then she liked it."

Do they consider their marriage equal or dominated by one or the other? Diane quickly answers, "I would have to say equal. Maybe from what we have said it doesn't sound that way, but I know that I always have had input into every decision. For instance, he really lost his shirt in a car dealership. He was immediately able to get a job selling cars in another car dealership, but I knew that that wasn't going to lead anyplace. I felt strongly that he needed to get out of that town and into some other kind of sales that I felt was more promising. So I literally forced him to write applications."

Herbert agrees, "And what happened was that one Sunday morning, she said, 'Okay, we're going to take the Sunday newspaper, and we're not going to bed until you've answered some ads.' And I got a job from it. I got out of the car business."

Although it was clear that Sam Simonian, at age seventy-nine, was economically in charge, he claims he and his wife are equal. He asserts, "I don't think there is a powerful one. There is an equal condition. Absolutely equal because there's such a tremendous force of respect. We don't say, 'I'm the boss and I make the decisions.' If her statement is right, I agree with her; she respects me. If my judgment is good, then she thinks that, too."

Some happily married couples in long-term relationships report that the husband is in charge. Hugh and Mary Carol O'Brien represent one such couple. Since her mother died when she was young, Mary Carol felt responsible for the other children. Until she met Hugh, she was highly career-oriented. Further, after the couple married, Hugh was away from home for two years in the navy. During this time, Mary Carol raised their first son alone. This combination of experiences encouraged Mary Carol to exercise more control and power than Hugh. Hugh denies that Mary Carol manages the relationship or the family. He explains, "I recognize her talents and she recognizes mine. No question, I was the head of the house, but I let her run things."

The O'Briens refer to Hugh as the "head" of the household and to Mary Carol as the "heart." While Mary Carol waxes eloquent on what this concept means to her, Hugh disagrees. He argues, "You make me sound like a king on a throne, and it hasn't been that way. We've had mutual respect." It was interesting that someone who is not in charge had the opportunity to define the power relationship between the two!

Ed Delaney is another man who is clearly in charge of his family. He asserts, "In our family, I make all of the big decisions. If we're going to invest money, where we go on trips, and buying homes, I decide. I make the big decisions. If we're going to buy a car, I want her to agree that she wants that car."

His friend, Tom Donahue, asks, "How do you do that? Do you twist her arm until she agrees?"

Ed explains, "I do that by looking at cars. She won't do the looking. I will. I'll go look at six different kinds of cars. She doesn't care that much. She doesn't want to get really deeply involved. Then I'll end up with a certain car, and I'll say, 'Let's go look at this car. I'd like to see it, if you'd like to see it.' She'll say, 'I want a white car. I don't care what else, but I want a white car.' So we get a white car. She decided. We go look at white cars in the kind of car I think I'd like to get. Then we decide, and she's in agreement."

Ed recalls another example. "Like the house we bought. I thought I would like it, but I didn't want to buy the house. I didn't say, 'Now we're going to buy this house.' I said, 'Let's go look at this house.' I was already in favor of it. It was necessary for me to get her agreement that she would like it."

His wife, Helen, offers this insight: "I'm pretty easy going. I like peace above everything else. A lot of things to me aren't worth arguing about."

Ed agrees, "Helen never gets in an argument."

True to form, Helen does not argue. "No, I don't. I can't stand arguments."

Ed reveals that he is strong-willed and dominant in the family. For her part, Helen notes that she has little power in the family and decides only what she wears. Even in her cooking, she tries to please her husband. She explains, "There are some things he knows that I don't—he graduated from college and I didn't." Helen concludes with a revelation. "If he had married someone like himself, it wouldn't have lasted at all."

Although Don Stouffer theorizes that success in marriage is dependent on "cooperation in everything you do and the decisions you make," in actual practice, Nancy often complies with his decisions. He admits, "I think she went along with me a lot more than I went along with her. We had some major decisions to make on real estate and investments. We started out with a fifty-dollar automobile and a couple of blankets and grew from there. If you don't work in the same direction, you're not going to attain."

Walter Clausen is very youthful in appearance. His wife, Laura, is slightly overweight and has cancer. Walter, rather than Laura, volunteered to talk about their long and happy marriage. In this way, they were consistent with most of the other couples. In general, the men, rather than the women, were eager to discuss their relationship. Although we might guess that women are more interested in relationships than men, this does not appear to be the case with older people. One explanation is the sex-role cross-over which begins at about forty years of age, when men become increasingly feminine and women become increasingly masculine.

Walter's phone call prompts me to ask, "Why were you motivated to call?" The answer allows an opportunity to explore the couple's relative power.

He responds, "I thought it was interesting; I thought you would be a very interesting person to meet. My wife kept putting the kibosh on it, but I said on Monday morning that I was calling."

Laura explains, "I think I was embarrassed, because I didn't think we had anything really important to say to you. I had read the article about your research, too, and I was impressed with the article and I was impressed with you. So, he won out."

Walter observes, "In that instance, I sort of ruled the decision-making process."

Laura adds, "He does a lot, though. But there's never any argument about it. The decisions he makes are always very wise."

Walter places trust in Laura's abilities. "But I think she could make good decisions if she wanted to."

Laura adds, with some insight, "Maybe it's because I don't want to."

Wife-dominated couples can also have a long and happy married life. Bill Cosby writes, "Any husband who says, 'My wife and I are completely equal partners' is talking either about a law firm or a hand of bridge. Yes, let us now set forth one of the fundamental truths about marriage: the wife is in charge. Or to put it another way, the husband is not."

Snookie Day tells a story of some friends who had just celebrated their fifty-eighth anniversary. The husband, Wilson, was asked the secret of the couple's success. He got up and slowly said, "It's very simple. Ellen does as she wishes. And I do as Ellen wishes." Snookie thinks his response is particularly humorous because the couple are both forceful people who have learned to live in great harmony.

Ivy and Ben Johnson, married fifty-two years, told a similar story. At their fiftieth wedding anniversary celebration, Ben was asked the same question. He responded, "If you want to have a long and happily married life, you only need to know two words, 'Yes, Dear.' "

The wife may be in charge of decision making, much to the satisfaction of both husband and wife. Perhaps Peg Adams is in charge because of her size—she stands six inches taller than her husband, Art. Although the couple had earlier suggested they are involved in "give and take," they agree that Peg makes most of the couple's decisions. Art illustrates, "When we bought our house, it was her idea. She wanted it, and it was okay with me."

Peg feels ambivalent about her decision-making role. She states, "He's very agreeable, he lets me have my way." On the other hand, she adds, "I get angry because he should learn how [to make decisions]." Even their daughter recognizes the father's dependence when she observes, "Ma, if something happens to you, I'm going to have double work."

Friends of happily married couples learn quickly that the dominant spouse likes to exercise domination outside the marriage as well as within it. The Delaneys have a husband-dominated marriage; the Donahues have a wife-dominated marriage. The two couples travel together, and the two dominant people—Ed Delaney and Ann Donahue—routinely do battle. Helen explains, "When we travel [the two couples together], those two [Ed and Ann] argue."

Tom Donahue agrees, "Ann and Ed argue about where they're going, how they're going to get there, what time it is. Helen and I just go along."

Ann explains, "I'm as outspoken as you (Ed) are, more so than Helen is, and when we're doing things, these two just sit back and let us decide. We're arguing about deciding, it has nothing to do with family."

Tom adds, "It has nothing to do with family. Ann decides most of the time if we're going to make a trip. She always plans ahead. Ann has a trick she plays. She says, 'In five months or six months.' I don't care what the hell is going to happen in five or six months. I'll promise to go anywhere. Just leave me alone. 'Can we go to New York in June?' 'Yeah, we'll go to New York.' "

Ann also handles the couple's finances. She relates, "Well, with the long hours, I got the financial end of it. We talked about it."

The Silvers are another wife-dominated couple. When they are asked if they made decisions based on their relative expertise, Ari responds quickly, "It's true we do that, and she has all of the expertise. She has the expertise at money, she has it in cooking. If I disagree about cooking, she thinks I'm a dope."

True to form, Ruth Ann disagrees, "No, I don't."

Ari provides an example. "If I say use more oil, you'll say, 'mind your own business.'"

Ruth Ann disagrees again. "No, I don't say that. I say, 'You're teaching me how to cook now?'"

• • •

Snookie is cross-sexed, in other words, a masculine woman. Although most women of her age did not go to college, she explains, "It never occurred to me not to go to college. I enjoyed school." In many ways, Snookie is ahead of her time. She competed in athletic events and won. She is assertive, straightforward, and lets other people know where she stands.

Snookie is an only child, but she feels that her personality was at least partly formed by Berea College and Berea Academy. She maintains that the academy and college were both forward-looking and sex-blind. Her mother, who died when Snookie was at Berea College, was also a strong and independent woman.

Acting like a boy, but being in a girl's body, created problems for her throughout her life. The most serious problem was with "Grandma," Duffy's mother, who was also a strong force. Although Snookie provides no single, telling incident, she summarizes that Grandma was always in competition for control with her. Grandma was eulogized at her funeral as someone who "was a woman of many faults, but great virtues." Snookie played her strength down when she was with Duffy's mother, but as Duffy said, "She could still sense it. She knew it instantly when she came into the room."

Duffy's mother was striking in appearance. She was over six feet tall at a time when people were far shorter than they are today. She had snow-white hair at the age of twenty-four. She wore men's shoes until she got out of college because they did not make size 11 1/2 shoes for women until then.

"Mother Day" looked very much like and was a close friend of Eleanor Roosevelt. The two were suffragettes together. Mother Day fought for Indian rights and set up opportunities for the Oneida Indians. She was a Democrat

in a Republican area, and she was with Eleanor at the White House on the weekend when Franklin Delano Roosevelt died at Hot Springs.

Duffy's father was a very quiet, loving perfectionist. He waited until he was thirty years of age to ask Duffy's mother to marry him. He believed in the "split pea theory," which suggests there is only one right woman for each man and one had to seek that perfect partner.

Duffy went from one dominant woman to another. He may be comfortable with Snookie because she is a familiar female type. However, Duffy's mother was forty-one when he was born and may have been less of a force in his life than she would have been if she had been younger when he was born. Duffy, like many other happy partners, is the youngest child in his family of origin.

• • •

Not only do happy couples vary in how they make decisions, they also show understanding and support in strikingly diverse ways. Most satisfied couples positively reinforce each other and confirm each other, but some do not, according to their own reports and in their actual interaction during the interviews. Nonetheless, even when such positiveness and support are not evident to an outside observer, partners interpret the spouse's behavior as positive.

Intimacy occurs in varying levels among satisfied couples. Some older couples are very close, while others are more moderate in their disclosures. Physical intimacy varies, too. The satisfied couples range from those who have very active sex lives, perhaps not as frequent in quantity but clearly as good or better in quality to those who no longer engage in sexual intercourse. Some who have no physical sex life do so because of physical inability, while at least one couple determines that "when you are an adult, you put away childish things."

Some couples have great autonomy and remain two separate individuals while others have become figuratively "one." Some of the more autonomous couples began their marriage as two separate beings and have retained their identity. Others became more independent in their later years. Some women began careers after their children were grown, which assisted in the independence they experience.

Conflict is viewed differently by satisfied couples. Some long-term marrieds avoid conflict; for others, it is a common occurrence. Although conflict may lead to the destruction of a family unit, it is the manner by which problems are solved in others, and is thus viewed as essential for the continuation of a satisfying family life. The happy couples represent the range from a near absence of fighting or bickering to a constant stream of verbal sparring.

Conflict resolution takes a variety of forms in the happy marriages, too. Although many happy couples suggest that "talking it out" is preferred, some use other methods to solve their problems. While couples do not resolve conflicts in the same ways, those with high marital satisfaction do manage their conflicts.

• • •

The Days' religious background is complex. Snookie identifies their affiliations. "My grandfather was a Methodist minister in Alabama and my great-grandfather was a Baptist minister, the good old hellfire-and-damnation kind in the South. So my family went to the Presbyterian church. I belonged to the Christ Union Church, in Berea, which is all faiths in one, which is how I grew up.

"When our five children came along they were all christened Episcopalian. We told them all through the years that it didn't matter what the name of the religion was as long as they had a faith. As a result we now have two Catholic nuns in the Sisters of Mercy, which is a working order. Both of them have been married. I always say no Day could be cloistered. One is a professor and the other is a psychotherapist. That's number one and number three. Number-two daughter is involved very deeply in the Unitarian church in Atlanta, Georgia. Number-four daughter is our one Episcopalian. She has even studied temporarily to become an Episcopalian minister. She is taking a sabbatical at the moment. With four children of her own, she has to concentrate on first things first. Number five is a Methodist."

Duffy's religious background is no less interesting. He was born in Oneida, New York, in the Oneida community. His grandparents were part of the community, which did not believe in civil marriage. Rather, everyone was married to everyone else through God. Consequently, his parents were born out of wedlock. After the community broke up, his father's parents did marry and had another child. His mother's parents died before they had the opportunity to legally marry.

Although the community did not believe in civil marriage, it encouraged education, and both of Duffy's parents attended college. His father, like him, went to Yale. Because of his parent's early life, religion was not an

28

important part of their life. Duffy recalls, "I asked them one time why we didn't talk religion. We talked sex, we talked gay things, but we never talked religion. They said we had too much of it. When the community broke up, we got exposed to so much of it, we just didn't bother." Duffy does not view himself as a religious person. When asked if he attends church, he responds, "Not if I can avoid it."

Snookie agrees that she does not attend church as much today as she did when the children were small. But she also feels obligated to defend Duffy. Snookie explains, "He doesn't have to be a structured Christian, he is a Christian."

Duffy goes on, "The kids are aware of all of this, and the two nuns are very concerned, because I've never been baptized and they are sure that I'm going you-know-where."

Many parents want their children to share their religious values and take them to church or synagogue regularly to encourage such habits in them. When these children reach majority, many drop away. Duffy and Snookie, by contrast, are somewhat laissez-faire about religion and have been rewarded with highly religious children in a variety of flavors. Could the secret to encouraging particular religious values be in allowing children to choose, rather than in imposing it on them?

Did Duffy and Snookie feel the dissolution of their daughters' marriages and their becoming nuns was stressful? Duffy claims it was, but Snookie asserts it was not. She describes it as a "learning experience." She continues, "It was not stressful. I have a faith, and they were following through on their own faith. Number one married a Catholic and converted to Catholicism. She wrote and asked us what we thought about it. We told her it was her life. She was twenty-four years old, and she was working on her doctorate. It was her life, not ours. She has been very happy. She gives me so much good feeling when we're around her. They're both—the two nuns—very happy and I think it's because it's working."

Snookie did say that when Christine—daughter number one—was given an annulment from her marriage, which included two sons, a certain amount of stress was involved. Christine did not become a nun immediately after the annulment; instead she waited until her children were more grown. The third daughter was working on her doctorate in psychology at the University of Munich when she met her husband, who was a psychiatrist. This couple lost a child and had no living children when she decided to become a nun. The two daughters are "very friendly" with their ex-husbands.

Did the Days continue to have children because the first four are daughters and only the last child is a son? To the contrary, they wanted to *have six daughters. Snookie recalls, "I made him promise I could have six daughters before we got married."*

• • •

A few years ago, Dr. Ruth became a household friend as she freely dispensed sexual advice to couples. Most important, she gave permission to couples to engage in those sexual practices that were satisfying to them. This book may serve the same function as it provides struggling couples with a variety of role models for happy, long-lasting marriages. No single model of communicative behavior defines the happy couple and distinguishes it from others who are more likely to be labeled "unhappy" or "dysfunctional."

Authors who suggest that happiness in marriage is dependent upon "three easy steps" or "four basic skills" are misleading, at best, and hurtful to those aspiring to marital happiness, at worst. Bill Cosby takes a humorous swipe at "Dear Abby's tips for brides on how to have a successful marriage." He observes, "There are no rules; you just have to wing it." The words of the happy couples introduced in this book lend credence to Cosby's humorous philosophizing.

Chapter 3

Lowered Expectations: "Shed a Few Tears"

It begins in delight and ends in wisdom.

—**Robert Frost**

Cookie Simonian is of medium height and is slightly overweight. Her face is smooth and attractive, encircled with striking gray hair, but the most noticeable feature is her large dark eyes, uncovered by glasses. She dresses in a strapless tan playsuit and gold slippers. Her nails are long, red, and freshly manicured. Around her neck she wears a necklace that has "Cookie" written in cursive. She is friendly, upbeat, and highly energetic.

Sam Simonian stands in the doorway of the patio, which adjoins the living area. The sun is on his back, so all you can see is the shadow of an imposing figure. As your eyes adjust, you view a ruggedly attractive man encircled by the blue of the sky and the Gulf of Mexico. Sam is dressed casually in a red Izod shirt and matching shorts. He wears tennis shoes and white socks. His open-necked shirt reveals a gold chain and thick, coarse black hair. His head is similarly covered with thick black hair, and he sports a dark and distinguishing moustache. His eyes, like Cookie's, are large and dark. Unlike hers, his are topped with dark eyebrows, which nearly meet above his nose.

He is attractive, and yet fear-inspiring. His large size, the blackness of his hair, his stance, and his silence are disquieting. At the same time, you feel attracted to this man. The attraction may be motivated by the same force that allows some female animals to enter estrus, or heat, only after the male has frightened them.

Cookie turned seventy-two in May, 1991, the same day she and Sam celebrated their fifty-second wedding anniversary. Although Cookie is seventy-two and Sam is seventy-nine years of age, neither look as though they have been married fifty-two years. Their energy, attitudes, and behaviors do not fit the stereotypes of people their age. They are rarely apart. They particularly enjoy dancing, traveling, backgammon, playing cards, and going on cruises. Their sexual appetite remains ravenous. They show no evidence of the stress that has marked their lives.

· · ·

The story is told of the local minister, who had preached that the Lord would always provide, who found himself in a flood. As he was hanging onto the front of his porch, a boat with some of his parishioners came by and they told him to jump on. The minister replied, "No, no, the Lord will provide." Another boat came along a little later as he was climbing onto his roof, but still he insisted, "No, the Lord will provide." As the minister was clinging to the top of his underwater home, a helicopter swooped down and the passengers entreated him to climb up the rope ladder to safety. The minister was firm, "The Lord will provide." Well, the flood raged on and the minister drowned. When he got to heaven he asked to see the Lord. When the Lord appeared, he said, "What happened? I've always preached that the Lord will provide. Where were you?" The Lord responded, "What are you talking about? I sent two boats and a helicopter." Perhaps if the minister had lowered his expectations, he would have been saved from an early death.

Similarly, couples fare better when they have lowered expectations for the relationship. People who go into marriage with high hopes and believe all of their dreams will come true may be disappointed or divorced. The greedy child whose long Christmas list is not filled is saddened even though he receives a pony for Christmas. The marital partner with great expectations is similarly crushed. On the other hand, the Christmas child who expects nothing is delighted by the smallest gift. The spouse with low expectations is delighted by each and every occasion that is something more than neutral.

Philosopher Harold Kushner, in his book *When All You've Ever Wanted Isn't Enough: The Search for a Life that Matters*, observes, "Nobody suffers in this world except people who want things they cannot have." He recommends, "When you learn not to desire, you will rise beyond suffering." Later he adds, "Instead of working so hard to raise the level of what you have to equal what you want, lower the level of what you want to that which you already have, or even lower, to the level of what cannot ever be taken away from you. Then instead of frustration and want, you will have tranquility and peace of mind."

Since many couples married forty to seventy years were married during the depression or the Second World War, they knew difficult times from the beginning. This hardship appears to have strengthened their marriages. For couples who began with virtually nothing, every accumulation is viewed positively. Carl Gronbeck, married forty-four years to Patricia, recalls their early days when they moved into an apartment in Chicago and had no furniture and no money. He states, "I went down the street to the furniture store. I told them who I was, that I had a job, but that I had no money. I asked if I could buy a bed on credit. The first store I went in, the people said no. So I said, 'Fine, I wanted to explain up front.' Why waste their time and mine? So I went into the next store, fully expecting to be thrown out of there. The man I talked with said, 'Go ahead.' Naturally, I picked out the best bed that he had. That's all we needed. All we needed was a bed. We got apple boxes for our table and chairs. When you don't have anything, anything that you have is a plus. If something tragic would happen and everything would be gone, as far as I'm concerned, I've lost nothing. I didn't have it before."

Carl Gronbeck sums up his feelings. "I look at my life today and look at our happiness, health, economic situation, family, and knowledge. I look back twenty years ago, and I say, 'I can't believe that that would happen.' You add it all up, I didn't think it was going to be there. Pure and simple, I've never been so happy in my life."

Mary Carol O'Brien, a college graduate with a degree in chemistry, married forty-nine years, tells a similar story. "We started out with nothing. Right out of college. My parents had died. His parents were 150 miles away. We were on our own. And everything we did, we did alone. We struggled alone. Our struggles together are what made us one."

Hugh, her inventor husband, agrees that being without family and being truly on their own made a difference in their early marriage. He asserts, "She couldn't go running home to mother. She had no mother to run home to. She didn't have a father, either. So we had to make things work. We didn't have much money, but we always had a job and we always had a home."

Will and Gladys Kennedy, former rest home operators from New Paris, Pennsylvania, married fifty years, have advice for couples just marrying. Gladys opines, "Don't expect it to be a bed of roses. It isn't. You just have to accept each other and respect their rights, which we have already done. He has certain things that I know he doesn't care about doing, and I never bellyache at him to do them. He doesn't like to wear neckties. He's always been a clean man, but he felt like a stuffed shirt when he had a necktie on, and he looked like it. You know he's not comfortable by looking at him. I don't insist he wear a tie."

Many people feel they become closer through hardships. Ernie and Phyllis Trent celebrated their fifty-second wedding anniversary on June 15, 1991. He was a machinist, and she was an elementary schoolteacher. They have three sons named Roger, Ronald, and Robert. The couple lived on the same property on which her parents and grandparents homesteaded in Lake Township, Michigan. They have never moved.

Ernie, seventy-five years old, is now retired. He loves fishing and wood carving. Not very long ago, he lost an eye. Ernie disclosed that he had had real difficulty adjusting to one eye, but that Phyllis had encouraged him to begin his normal activities again. Shortly afterwards, he and Phyllis joined an Air Stream caravan and went fishing in Canada. Ernie went to get groceries on the trip, slipped on some melted ice, and splintered his wrist bone. He laments, "That took care of the fishing, and that took care of the carving."

Phyllis, a former school teacher, philosophizes, "But he could do it with the other hand. You can adapt. People can adapt if they make their mind up. I think we build our own mountains."

Rudy Bemke describes an accident in which he was involved. Six weeks after moving to Detroit, he was struck down by a truck. Unconscious for ten days, Rudy was not expected to live. Katrina remarks, "You have to have some of this adversity to give your life real meaning and to decide what's important and what isn't."

Writer Harold Kushner asks, "Will someone to whom things came effortlessly in youth ever learn the disciplines of patience and postponing gratification, or will that person be unprepared for the day when the music stops and people start saying no?" His question is relevant to those seeking long and happy marriages in the last decade of the twentieth century. Were people married forty to seventy years ago satisfied because they began with so much less than people who marry today?

Risk-taking marks many happy marriages. For instance, Jackie Stanowski, a former hospital bookkeeper from Three Rivers, Massachusetts, recalls, "George said, 'What do you think if I quit the shop and go full time [in the private cement business he had begun on the side]?' I was pregnant with my first child at the time. I said, 'What have you got to lose? Either I'll go to work or you will.' So he tried it, which a lot of people are afraid to do. I hear a lot of people say, 'I'd love to be self-employed.' But that is a big risk. What have you got to lose? If you fall on your face, you go to work someplace else. So he took the chance."

Carol Rubin, a psychologist in private practice, and Jeff Rubin, a psychologist at Tufts University, provide advice on how people might be happier during the Christmas season. One of their suggestions is "try to lower lofty expectations. Head off for the Christmas visit expecting to have a passable, but not wonderful time."

Couples who wish to be happy may follow the same advice. Los Angeles psychologist Sylvia Weishaus, who has studied those married fifty years and more, suggests that couples who marry should not "cling to unrealistic hopes." She advises that people should "forget the spouse makeover. If he doesn't dance the tango or she hates weekends in the woods, find a way to live with it." If you only expect a passable marriage, you may end up with lasting love.

• • •

The energetic Armenians, the Simonians, ooze sensuality. What first attracted them to each other? Sam begins a long story. "I used to sing in the Armenian church choir. They were giving us a shindig."

Cookie continues, "My mother heard there was going to be a concert, and she came home and said to my sister and I, 'Why don't you two join that concert?' We gave a concert in Watertown, and Sam was there. He saw me up on the stage."

Sam resumes, "Our church group all had previous dates, but we always did everything together. That day we went to the concert. After the concert we went to an ice cream parlor. Everybody had dates. I said, 'You guys didn't tell me about dates, but you know something? In that group of singers there was a girl who attracted me very much. She had a black velvet dress on. She was gorgeous. Who is she? Her figure!' One of the guys said, 'Forget her—her father is an old-fashioned guy. You'll never get her.' I said, 'Just tell me who she is, what's her name, and give me one hour's time.' I found out who she was, and I called her up. She wasn't home so I called her up again, and she was home. I told her who I was. I asked her to go with us and she said, 'Yes.' I went down and picked her up.

"My mother-in-law was the sweetest woman in the world. I enjoyed her very much, but she died very young. My father-in-law was an old-fashioned guy. He didn't care about dates. In our country, they make our dates. They arrange the marriage. He wasn't that bad, but he knew about arranged dates. If you had seen my wife in the early age! She had the figure. She had curly hair that you couldn't imagine, long, curly hair. She had gorgeous, big, beautiful eyes. As we get older our bodies shrink, but in my mind I'm always thinking how Cookie was. For instance, I have one particular scene in my mind. She wore this big, long white hat on the boardwalk in Atlantic City at one time. She's walking on the boardwalk. I can never take that scene out of my mind. Certain things always stay in your mind and you always think about that."

Cookie adds some information. "We met about October. We got engaged May 20, my birthday, and we got married in August. In less than a year."

Sam brags, "And we had a child nine months after we got married. There was a baby boy."

Cookie smiles, "He was born two minutes past midnight on May 21, and we were married August 20. On my twenty-first birthday, I was in labor."

Was it love at first sight? Sam answers quickly, "Mine was. I saw her and I was very attracted. We went and had ice cream. I couldn't leave her alone. She wanted to go with this group to New York. I didn't want her to go."

Cookie explains, "It was a concert."

Sam recalls, "She was like telling me, 'Well, I'm going anyway.'"

Cookie notes, "He said to me, 'If you go to the concert in New York, then I'll never see you again.' I said, 'That's all right.' I did go, but my mother said, 'Don't go, he's too good.' I didn't know what love was. When he said to me 'Do you love me?' I said, 'I don't know.' He said, 'Do you like me?' I said, 'Yes.' He said, 'Well, that like is going to grow into love.' Those are just the words he used to me. That's the way he proposed to me. In those days, when a person took out an Armenian girl to a formal, that meant something. As he was leaving my house, he turned around and started singing to me. I thought 'we just met, and he already took me to a big, formal affair.' I thought, 'This is it.' "

• • •

The Roman Leo Salerno is predictably poetic: "Old age is not all that glitters. Instead of doing the two-step, you decide you're going to waltz." Happy couples are not free from stress and problems. Many of them face serious problems, but weather the storm. As one person notes, "No one cares how many storms you encountered, it's whether you brought the ship home."

Stress is inevitable among spouses. Couples experience disruptive and disquieting influences and life events and related hardships that are serious enough to create change in the family. These events may be viewed objectively as positive—the purchase of a new home, the building of a new home, or the addition of a baby to the family—or as negative—the death of a family member, an extended illness of a child, or the failure to gain a promotion at work.

Stress is present at one point or another for all couples. Stress is related to a variety of health problems, including cardiovascular problems and cancer. However, it is welcomed by those who enjoy changes in their life and are bored when events are not in flux.

New Yorkers Ruth Ann and Ari Silver engage in a great deal of bantering, arguing, and interrupting. As an outsider, you might conclude that their relationship is always stressful; however, it appears that the unique interaction they have developed works for them. Sometimes it is difficult to know if Ari is joking or is serious. Consider this exchange.

Ruth Ann explains, "My father understood the urgency of our desire to get married. He said okay. There was no argument."

Ari adds, "He not only said, 'Okay,' he said, 'October 10.' "

Ruth Ann details her father's actions. "Well, he got up and called a rabbi and set a date."

Ari repeats, "He said, 'October 10.' "

Ruth Ann continues, "That's how you do it."

Ari maintains, "That's how a father does it who wants to get rid of his daughter."

Ruth Ann disagrees, "My father had one child, and I was it. Believe me, I was the apple of his eye."

Ari acquiesces, adding, "That was very true, but your mother was very anxious for you to get out of the house."

Ruth Ann's mood suddenly changes. "Yes, dear," she says, "whatever you say. That's the secret of a happy marriage: 'Yes, dear.' "

Ari continues, "She was very jealous of her, actually she was."

Ruth Ann clarifies, "Not at that point. Only after we were married, and you climbed up the corporate ladder and began to indulge me with all sorts of wonderful things."

What was the most stressful period in their marriage? Ari answers, "Very early in our marriage. You see, I spent a great deal of time with my family because they were very dependent on me. Ruth Ann resented it, and it caused a lot of stress. She didn't want me to spend any time with my family. She had gotten me away, and she wanted me out of the family. This caused her a lot of grief and me a lot of aggravation. It became a very sore spot, and it lasted until my family died."

Ruth Ann explains, "They were not as dependent on him as they led him to believe they were."

Ari disagrees, "Oh, really? They were immigrants, and they had problems."

Ruth Ann snaps, "They got here without you."

Ari continues, "They couldn't have made it without me."

Ruth Ann ends the conversation. "We're not going to fight that fight again," she says.

How long was this stressful period? Ari asserts, "It lasted from the day we were married until the day they both died." How long was this period? Although the couple could not agree on how long it was—Ari thought it lasted forty years, and Ruth Ann thought it lasted twenty years—they compromised on twenty-five years.

Ruth Ann notes that for all outside appearances, she and Ari's mother got along. They talked to each other on the phone each day, they went shopping together, and they told each other jokes. However, she adds, "There was an underlying resentment on both our parts. Because she was taking him away from me, and she, because I was taking him away from her. We were fighting the same battle."

Ari asserts, "There was no problem with her family because they didn't care."

Ruth Ann quickly defends her family. "Oh, they cared. But my father thought it was very normal for a daughter to marry and leave home."

Ari interprets her family's behavior. "And they were very independent. They were an independent couple. They didn't need us."

Ruth Ann returns to Ari's family. "My mother-in-law thought 'my son is my son, my only son,' " she says. "She called him 'her pearl.' Does that give you the picture?"

Ari's family was clearly dependent on him. Every time he and Ruth Ann moved, they moved his family as well. Each time, they would purchase a home for themselves and a nearby home for his parents. Surprisingly, the two couples never lived under the same roof.

Stress occurs in response to life and family developments, and it also occurs as a result of less predictable events. Developmental stress is particularly salient during the early marital years, when a baby is added, during middle age, and in later years. Two psychologists, Lazarus and DeLongis, explain:

> . . . we must see people as engaged in a life drama with a
> continuous story line that is best grasped not as a still photo
> but as a moving picture with a beginning, middle, and end.

Couples identify different developmental periods as the most difficult for them. The most stressful period for many occurred early in their marriage when they were poor, faced the depression, or dealt with the Second World War. Yet this trial by fire bonded the couples for life.

Leo Salerno identifies the beginning of his marriage during World War II as the worst time. "We were young, and I had just pledged to go to college, and Uncle Sam said 'I want you.' Kids couldn't to go Canada in those days. You couldn't run away from it. Everyone was patriotic, we did our thing.

"It was difficult because when I went overseas it was hard on her. And being only twenty years old, at that time, getting in a shooting war, it was hell. It was hard on me doing what I had to do in the war, and it was hard on her being alone. We had just gotten married, we just got to know each other, and all of a sudden the war came along, and now we're apart.''

Courtney agrees that it was the most difficult period of their marriage for her as well. But neither of the two felt that things immediately improved when Leo came home from the war. Leo recalls, ''The postwar was tough because we had a recession. You went back to your own job, but you weren't prepared for it. There was trauma. Jobs were hard to come by, and starting out all over again, and getting started in your marriage again. Financially, it was tough. '47, '48, '49, '50, it was hard to get started.''

Courtney adds, ''We did without an awful lot.''

Other couples had difficulty during the first years of marriage as a result of adjusting to marriage and each other. The war and financial problems were less relevant than the normal adjustment of a traditional working husband and a traditional homemaking wife.

Ed Delaney, the youngest child in his original family, is now seventy-five. He looks thoughtful. ''The worst time? We used to fight, the first year, when we lived in the army. She was home all day, resting, eating bonbons. I was running up and down the fields. I was in the infantry. Up and down, up and down, out in the hot sun in Mississippi and Louisiana all day long. Come home at night, and you're exhausted. She'd say, 'You don't love me. You don't love me.' She'd want to go out and dance.''

His wife, Helen, the oldest of her siblings, is now seventy-two. She agrees, ''I wanted him to play soldier all day, and dance all night, I guess.''

Ed considers this. ''I didn't really feel like saying it was off forever and ever. But I thought, and I told her, 'Why don't you get on the train and go home?' ''

Helen disagrees, ''I don't think so. I don't think so.''

Ed persists, ''Yes, you said, 'I think I will.' But she never did. There were a few days like that. Because that was really tough. You're up at five in the morning. The pressure of up and down hills all day long, in the hot sun. Getting home at 6:00 or 6:30. We had to stay for the officers' mess. When that was over, there were a couple of speeches, and I was one of the speakers. I'd get home at seven o'clock, and she'd been home eating bonbons all day. She was completely rested, and I was completely exhausted. That was the worst time.''

Helen is petulant. ''I haven't told about my hard times.''

Ed adds, "We never talked about splitting up, but we thought maybe she would go home, send her home. I had six days a week anyway. Fourteen hours a day, and she was sitting home watching TV or whatever you watch in those days, radio, I guess. Those were very stressful times."

• • •

Sam Simonian is the oldest child in his original family while Cookie is the youngest. He was born in Armenia, and his early experiences and religion were important in shaping the man that he has become. After his initial silence, Sam becomes effusive. He recalls his birth and childhood. "I was born in Armenia in a very wealthy family. I was born in a fifty-seven room castle. Between 1915 and 1918, the Turks massacred all the Armenians.

"The Turks massacred all the Armenians and took everything that they owned. They took them to the deserts to kill them—millions and millions of people. Fortunately, somebody that knew my grandfather well came into the caravan in the desert where all the Armenians were being held. This man gave a few gold pieces to the soldiers and asked if there were any Simonians in this particular area. He explained he would like to take them with him to his home to serve him. We went to his house, and he sheltered us and saved us.

"Later we came to America. My father was in the United States and had gone through the depression. He had money and he invested it, but then he lost it. So we started from a very rich family and became very poor. I didn't have one day of school when I came to America. Not even one day. There was no school, no church. Everything had been destroyed. So anything my mother could teach us—just a little bit—that's all that we knew.

"So when I came to America, the first thing I had on my mind was that I must have some kind of formal education. I began in first grade, grammar school. Within four years from the day I came to America, I was graduated from high school. I wanted success in my life. I didn't want my family to ever be poor.

"I went into the dry cleaning business, and many years later I had a big success. I built a big plant from nothing. My son and my brother were partners with me. When I gave the business to my children sixteen years ago, my son asked me what advice I could give him. I said, 'The only advice I could give you is be honest to yourself.'"

• • •

Some stress occurs because of less predictable events. Family researcher Walsh calls these "the slings and arrows of outrageous fortune." Such events may be positive or negative and include both chronic and terminal illnesses, unexpected or untimely deaths, unexpected promotion or demotion at work, surprising windfalls of resources or personal accomplishments, and wars or national events.

Susie Callahan, who has lived most of her forty-four-year marriage in Boston, discloses that the worst times she and her husband experienced were related to finances. "It was about three or four years ago. We bought the Dairy Queen downtown across from the hospital, and everything was fine. Business increased. We brought in new customers, and we were doing real well. Then he developed a bad back."

Jim, who was a steel mill executive, continues, "I had a bad back, but it got worse. Along with being in excruciating pain all the time, it affected my personality."

Susie does not disagree. "He was miserable. He was in so much pain all the time."

Jim adds, "I was very quick with her. I took it out on her and on the business."

Susie notes, "It was the least money we've ever had."

Jim reminds her, "We lost an awful lot of money in that big development, too. We lost everything. I had no pension. That was in 1980 when interest rates were very different than now. I decided to leave the steel business. The steel business was going down the tube. It was in real bad shape. It was an ideal time to get out. A bunch of guys got together and invested. We invested, and we developed a project. We were going to build sixteen townhouses, duplexes, apartments around a ten-acre lake. They asked me to come down to Florida and do it for them. I said, 'Gee, this is an ideal time to get out of the steel business, and come down here.' So we did. At the time we got involved, the interest rates were like 10 1/8. By the time we got the first duplexes built, they were 19 1/2. Now how do you sell anything at 19 1/2 percent interest? It was a wipeout!"

What is the most difficult age when raising children? Parents of infants identify that period, while parents of teenagers claim their plight is worse. One couple shared that parenting when the children are in their late forties is the worst! Regardless of the most difficult phase, a number of couples identify problems with their children after the children had left home as causing the most stress in their marriages.

Carl and Patricia Gronbeck, parents of two sons, age forty-three and thirty-five, and one daughter, who is forty, had a particularly difficult time when their daughter quit college and went to Florida to work. Although they had visited her in Florida shortly before, they talked her into coming home and returning to college. She obliged, but after she had been home one day, she announced that she had given birth to a baby the week before. They had no idea, even though they had seen her two months before. The daughter was twenty-one, and told her parents that she wanted to bring the baby home, rather than give it up for adoption.

Patricia admits, "I was a basket case for a couple of hours. It was no problem for Carl. He said, 'We'll just have to go get the baby.' Now she's the joy of our life. It was a hard time, but it didn't last more than a couple of weeks. Once the baby was here, we were fine. It's your pride that's hurt in a small town. I was teaching by then. After awhile, you just say, 'This is the way it is.' "

More recently, events in this daughter's life have created stress for the Gronbecks. Their daughter met a man who was an attorney who had never been married. The three—the daughter, Karen; the grand-daughter, Melanie; and David, the new man—got along perfectly. All of the in-laws liked and respected each other. Karen's brothers jokingly commented, "David makes us look bad!" Karen and David were married and appeared to be in wedded bliss for a number of years. Carl and Patricia visited them in a beautiful new home and were happy to see how well the family got along. They felt they could finally breathe a sigh of relief as far as Karen was concerned.

One week after the visit, Karen called to say that David had left her. While they were married, he had had two separate affairs. He had decided to leave her for one of these other women. Patricia reminisces, "David just made you feel wonderful. Unfortunately he must have done that with a lot of people." Melanie was in high school, and was particularly upset by the leaving of the only man she had known as a father.

Their other children have also caused stress for the Gronbecks. Their older son and daughter-in-law have had marital problems, and their younger son moved in with them for awhile because he could not find work. The same son traveled to Israel and called his parents to say that he had met a woman and was not coming back home; he was going to remain on a kibbutz. Fortunately for the Gronbecks, the officials would not enroll their son in the University of Jerusalem so he was essentially forced to return home. Patricia smiles, "Right now we're stress-free for a few minutes. We always said that they take turns. First it was one, then the other. Then the good one was good, and the bad one wasn't quite as good."

Not only do couples' children create unpredicted stress, so do aging parents. The Bemkes, community-minded folks who never had children, experienced stress because of Katrina's aging mother. Rudy begins hesitantly, looking at his wife, "I suppose there was a stretch. . . ."

Katrina admits, "I had a lot of trouble with my mother."

Rudy corrects, "I was going to say, the only problems we've had were with each other's family. When my dad was sick, my mom took care of him; and when he died, she went all to pieces. We just thought it was old age. She really had a terribly serious mental breakdown, and it took us several years to catch it. We lived next door to the doctor. I called him one day, and he said we had to change her medicine. So they changed her medicine and within five days, she was normal.

"Her mother lived 165 miles away from us. We went to see her every weekend—our weekends, to see her mother."

Katrina adds, "We would take her a new dress."

Rudy repeats, "Take her a new dress."

Katrina continues, "And she'd throw it at us."

Rudy recalls, "Or she'd throw it in the corner. Take her a box of candy, and she'd flush it down the toilet. All those nice things. But we were taking our time—to drive up, and stay overnight in a motel that we didn't want to be in. She'd come home crying. I'd come home dead as a drum. So there were a lot of holidays we spent trying to pacify these families."

Katrina observes, "At the time we were doing what we had to do for ourselves. That's right. That's the only way you can look at this. Rather than wish five years later that you had done it. But it is tough. That's really hard. It's tough."

A surprising number of happy couples reveal that depression, manic-depressive bouts, or other mental illness occurred in their long marriage. Although Molly Frost identifies the most stressful time in their marriage as when the children left home, her husband David, a sixty-four-year-old newspaper advertising manager, tells another story. He recalls, "There was a period of time where she had acute depression, and that was tough. I had difficulty handling that. It didn't last very long."

Molly recalls the time. "I would wake up with this black cloud over my head, and it would just stay there. Nothing felt good. I was trying desperately to take care of the children, and everything was just a tremendous job. The kids were preschool, first grade, second grade. I'd like to forget that. It was tough. The kids were little, and they sensed something was wrong. I think I've tried to forget that. I think the cause was chemical imbalance, a hormonal type thing."

Her husband reveals, "I'm not sure how stressful that was for her, but it was for me. I was doing everything I could—slapping her once—and that hurts when I say that. But I tried everything else. One day she didn't want to get out of bed, at all. I told her, 'Somebody's gotta take care of these kids.' I'd tried everything else, and I don't think I slapped her too hard—I hope."

Molly looks surprised. "I don't recall that. I've blocked that out."

David tries to prompt her memory. "You were wearing a black nightgown."

Molly looks perplexed. "I don't remember that."

They both laugh, and David concludes, "She can't even remember owning a black nightgown!"

Continuing in a serious tone, he adds, "But that was stressful, it really was. I was afraid to leave her. But I see that as very narrow, not more than a couple of years. It was a very narrow period where it was that stressful. I felt like it was somehow my fault. In some way, I'm creating this, and what can I do about it? I wanted to fix it."

Alexander Smith, the youngest child among his siblings, is now sixty-nine years old. He retired from the corporate headquarters for Sears, Roebuck & Company after thirty-seven years with them. He went through a long period of depression as a result of job difficulties.

His wife, Peggy, a former secretary and bookkeeper, is seventy-one. She recites, "Lots of times, I can remember, we'd sit down to breakfast, and I would pray before he went to work. He couldn't eat, yet I could. I was just more concerned about getting him out of that depression than anything else. I could pray about it out loud so that he knew that I was praying for him. Of course, I prayed lots of times when he didn't."

Alexander explains the provocation. "My boss was a three-star general in the marines, and I was not in the service. I sometimes wondered why he ever brought me into the firm. All of the men, almost without exception, were either marines, army, or navy. I had been in the department for seven years as an assistant. I had moved around; I got a raise all the time.

"The boss met a man at the Marine Reserve Corps meetings that he took a shine to, a man who had been with Sears, but had left, and was managing a photographic store down in Chicago. He encouraged Homer to go with Sears, and Mr. Peacher hired him straight into the corporate headquarters, in our department. It was strictly against his former rule. He always said that you had to have field experience. You had to manage a department."

Alexander detailed all of the special favors received by this new hire. At the same time, his own career slowed down and the less experienced colleague was promoted ahead of him. He was deeply depressed for six months. One day he decided the depression was over. "Thank God, six months later, I was promoted from that job to another job. Then things went straight up."

The couples' physical and mental illnesses were not the only source of unpredicted stress. Many reported that their children had chronic or acute illness that created problems for the family. The Clausen family provides an illustration. Laura Clausen, mother of two daughters, relates the story of their first daughter's birth. "Sherry was born the ninth of June and she was born with a birth defect. We were young; this was our first baby."

Her husband, Walter, adds, "And I was graduating from dental school."

Laura shares her memories. "I'm in the hospital with a baby that has a birth defect. About two weeks after she is born, Walter has to report to naval duty. I was left with my parents, who were very, very good, and then my parents took me out to Washington, D.C., to be with him. That's how we started out our marriage."

Walter agrees, "There's no doubt that was very stressful."

Together they tell the story. Laura begins, "She has had a lot of surgery. She was born with her bladder on the outside."

Walter adds a relevant fact. "It happens in one in every 350,000 babies."

Laura specifies, "She had the first surgery when she was nine months, then again at eighteen months. We were in the navy at the time. She had surgery again at three. They transplanted the ureters. Her bladder was like it had been sliced open and laid out. So you could see the ureters. They couldn't just open her up, and put that back in. She had no urethra, either. Congenitally, she was missing that.

"They did what they called a urethra transplant. They transported those ureters into her lower colon at the age of eighteen months. They left the bladder, and we went to Hawaii. We came back, and stopped at San Francisco, and the surgeon removed the bladder. We started across the United States with a little toddler with an incision that was wide open. We made it back, and we had Joan by then.

"Sherry went along, and they did some plastic surgery when she was seven. I said to the surgeon, 'Oh, everything is going to be just fine now.' He looked me right square in the eye, and he said, 'Just about the time you think everything is going to be okay, it may all blow up.' His words were to come to pass.

"When she was a freshman in college, she had six kidney stones. She had two in the kidney and four in the ureter, hooked right up where the ureter emptied into the colon. That colon produces a pouch. She was in the hospital a month, the month of June. My mother died in March, and my father died in October, and Sherry spent the month in the hospital. So that was very stressful, too. A very tough year. That was '69.

"She was married in '72 and in '75, she had another kidney stone, and she ended up being in the hospital another month. Both times she was in the hospital that long because she developed an abscess from the kidney stone when they went in to remove it. Now they've had her on medication, and that was '75, and this is '89; she's had fourteen good years. They finally have her on a medication that seems to prevent these kidney stones."

Laura moves to the present. "She [Sherry] is an interesting girl because she doesn't ever want us to talk about it. She has a compulsion for life. I said to her one day, 'Sherry, I don't know how you keep the pace you keep.' She said, 'Well, I might not live very long, and I'm going to live every day to the fullest, and I'm going to do everything.' "

Walter wisely adds, "When you think about those stressful times, in your early life, you were able to cope with those easier than you are at our ages now."

• • •

Throughout their marriage, Sam was self-employed in the dry cleaning business while Cookie was a housewife. The couple had four children, but lost a daughter, at 6 1/2 years of age in a swimming accident. Sam and Cookie were vacationing alone, and other family members were caring for their oldest, and at the time, only child. Cookie remembers stoically, "I never show my feelings. In fact when we lost my daughter, he almost had a nervous breakdown. My daughter drowned with her first cousin. Both clung together because neither of them knew how to swim. We weren't there; we had gone on vacation. My daughter had gone with my mother-in-law, father-in-law, and my brother-in-law, and they had gone to a beach, to a lake. My brother-in-law let the two children go into the water by themselves while he went off, and they were both drowned. One was 6 1/2 and one was 7 1/2."

• • •

Others also experienced one of the ultimate stressful events in the death of a child. Peggy and Alexander Smith, married forty-eight years and from Glen Ellyn, Illinois, lost their first child under tragic circumstances. Alexander relates, "The worst time was when we lost Dickie. Dickie was born with organic brain damage, and we had him at home up until he was five, and then we had to put him in [an institution] when Shirley came along. It was too much of a chore for Peg. So we had to put Dickie in a special school. He died rather tragically."

Peggy continues, "He swallowed a stone. It got lodged and he couldn't get it up."

Alexander details, "Early evening, before they put him down to bed. They found him out on the grounds turning blue, and they thought he had pneumonia. They rushed him to the hospital, and found a stone lodged in his esophagus. They couldn't get it out, they had to force it down. Then he contracted pneumonia. He could be alive today. There wasn't anything physically wrong."

Peggy reminisces, "He was a beautiful little boy. He had blonde, curly hair and blue eyes. He was a beautiful child."

Alexander provides more detail. "Every Wednesday, I was off at the store, and we used to take him to a special school in St. Louis where a cousin of hers worked, where they dealt with these kind of children. He seemed to be making progress, but they finally said there was no more they could do. It was stressful because he used to have convulsions when he was home."

Peggy defends the boy's memory. "There were lots of good times with him, though. He was a very affectionate, lovable little boy. He just couldn't get enough love. He'd crawl up on your lap, he'd just cuddle up, and like to be loved all the time. We had lots of fun times that we enjoyed, and yet behind all of that was the thought that we can't go on, and what are we going to do when he gets older? That was taken care of for us, but that was a difficult thing. I think the hardest thing we ever did was take him to that school."

Alexander concurs, "To walk away, and leave him there was tough."

Peggy explains the circumstances of admitting Dickie to the institution. "It got to a point one time where in the night, I had fed Shirley. I was nursing her, so I fed her and then got back to bed. I had been there, I don't think ten minutes, and I heard Dickie, and he had a convulsion. I got up with him, and got him calmed down and over it, and then I fell apart. Alexander called my doctor. We found out later that the doctor had written to this school and had said, 'Either you take this child or the mother.' "

Alexander adds, "We had made an application and were on the waiting list to get in."

Peggy owns up to her behavior. "I couldn't stop crying, I couldn't stop shaking. The doctor had said, 'You take the child or you're going to end up with the mother.' "

Couples in happy marriages experience unpredicted stressful events just as do people in less satisfied marriages. The difference between those who are blissfully wed and those who are not may be how they define these events. Harold Kushner, in his well-known book *When All You've Ever Wanted Isn't Enough,* observes, "Expecting the world to treat you fairly because you are a good person is like expecting the bull not to charge you because you are a vegetarian." The happily married couples had no expectations that they would be free from problems and unexplainable stressful events.

Couples in lasting, satisfying marriages respond differently to changes that occur within their life than couples in dissatisfying marriages. Some research shows that individuals who learned how to cope with stress early in their life may be better able to cope with problems later on. Many of the couples interviewed learned about stress in their earliest days together.

Irwin Sarason, an important researcher on stress, explains that coping with stress requires people to set aside unproductive concerns and to deal with problems. His advice is similar to the often-quoted prayer "Lord give me the courage to change the things I can, the serenity to accept the things I cannot, and the wisdom to know the difference."

Other investigators coin the terms *crisis-proof family* and *energized family,* describing those families that are unlikely to become unstable when faced with major changes. Such families are characterized by flexible relationships and a shared sense of power. Adaptability is a major consideration in successful models of marital satisfaction. Problem-solving abilities may help families cope with changes. Finally, social networks, including friends and extended family members, are of increased importance during times of stress.

Couples use both internal and external means of coping with stress. The internal strategies include redefining the stressful event so it is more manageable and attempting to view the stressful event as less important by determining a positive response to it.

The Gronbecks used these methods in dealing with stressful experiences. Carl Gronbeck's approach was somewhat novel. As an insurance person, he realized the financial difficulties people can face. When one of the children or grandchildren had a problem, he is most likely to solve it with an insurance policy or an investment. For instance, when his daughter, Karen, divorced, his first thought was to get an insurance policy for Melanie, the granddaughter. He explains, "I know it sounds crazy, but I bought a life policy for Melanie. If something happened to me, there is going to be enough seed money so she can go to college. The whole idea is you devise a plan economically for all the kids to be well taken care of."

For the Nortons, both youngest children in their original families, no change was too major if it resulted in relieving their stress. Diane Norton explains that they moved across the country from Minnesota to Florida as a result of her husband's stress at work. "The job was stressful, and we had come down here on vacation, and the climate seemed absolutely marvelous, as far as he was concerned. His skin gets terribly dry up North. He was so much more comfortable down here."

She adds, "But one thing neither of us believes in are moods, or being moody. We really think that's a cop-out. It distresses us if one of our kids would say, 'Oh, today was a bummer!' I don't believe you have any right to say that. I think you should really try to be tough."

Darlene Dahlquist is a woman who has had open-heart surgery but still smokes cigarettes and seeks adventures. She describes stress as creating "a whole new adventure." She asserts, "Stress is, for your information, what I think a strong marriage is all about. We never had time to make a mountain out of a molehill. Sure, we had lots of problems. We had lots of heartaches. But another thing would come up, and you had to go on to the next thing. There's no way you could avoid it. You couldn't dwell on what happened. You just kept on going. One year led to another, and I said, 'I can't believe it. I can't believe it's forty-two years.' And, we're not old. Our kids—my God, when I think this one's thirty-five, that one's thirty-six, and that one's thirty-nine. Can you believe that? I look in the mirror, and I think, 'Gee whiz.' "

After discussing her illnesses and potential death, she remarks, "It's part of the deal. Right now I feel that we have had a wonderful, full life. The kids are grown, they're well fixed. Leonard is old enough to take care of himself. Everybody's born to die. I keep telling him that, and I keep telling the kids that.

"Don't mourn. Shed a few tears to get it out of your system, but just try to remember when Grandpa [Darlene's dad] died having a cocktail with me. It was a shock to everybody, but it was the best way to go. Remember Grandma, two years ago, who lingered and suffered? Which way would you like me to go? In the night, bad heart, drop dead, or what? Just think of it that way, and that's the way I believe.

"I went for my bypass surgery. My doctor was annoyed with me because I said, 'Just remember, if I can't use any of my organs for anything, you can certainly use my eyes.' He said, 'Who said you're going to die?' You know they want you to have a positive attitude. I just said, 'You have to help other people when you're gone. Sight will help somebody. Take my eyes.' "

External approaches to relieving stress include gaining social support from friends and family, finding spiritual support from the clergy, and using community resources, including social service agencies and educational opportunities. These methods are used by satisfied couples.

The Smiths, the Baptist couple from Illinois who institutional-ized their son and eventually lost him to an unusual accident,

51

turned to their religion. Peggy looks back. "Faith in God, our religion. We were in a small church, and the pastor and his wife were very, very good to us and helped us tremendously. In fact, they went with us, they drove when we had to take Dickie to the school so we would not have to go alone. They were with us then, and so were our other friends."

Alexander adds, "Their daughter—the daughter of the pastor and his wife—used to babysit for us so we could get away. Our daughter, Shirley, was named after their daughter."

Peggy reaffirms, "I would say the only way we got through was our friends and our religious faith. I had wonderful in-laws who treated me like I was their own. I couldn't have had better, more loving in-laws than I had. They were wonderful. They were there to help. Lots of family and lots of friends. It makes a difference."

What can we conclude about a couple's coping skills? First, the couple may be better able to cope with a stressful situation if they perceive it as less rather than as more severe. The meaning the couple attaches to the event is critical in determining how they will experience it and how they will cope with it. Second, discussing the stressful situation in order to gain a shared social meaning may render it more understandable and solvable. Specific coping strategies vary among different families.

Couples with lowered expectations are happier than those with heightened aspirations. Happy couples experience stressful events, just as unhappy couples do. The difference between the two is their ability to cope with the predictable and unpredictable events that life presents. In the next chapter, you will learn that people in long, happy marriages not only accept their spouse's idiosyncrasies, but they come to appreciate them!

Chapter 4

Unconditional Acceptance: "I Love Your Bony Knees"

Love is what happens to men and women who don't know each other

—**W. Somerset Maugham**

Ben Neilsen looks like a tall Ichabod Crane. He is very thin and angular. His hands and feet are long and narrow. Although he is not clumsy, he looks awkward because of his dimensions. Ben sports a full beard, and both his hair and beard are dark, streaked with some gray. His silver-framed glasses pick up the highlights in his hair. When we first meet, Ben is dressed casually in blue and white striped seersucker pants, a light blue button-down collar oxford cloth shirt, white sports socks, and no shoes.

Julia is similarly tall, but does not look awkward. She is a large-boned woman of average weight for her height and structure. She has short gray hair and brown round-rimmed glasses. She is dressed in a light blue and white striped casual shirt, white full walking shorts, and multicolor sandals. Both she and her husband are relaxed and casual in their attire as well as their demeanor. They have been married forty-seven years.

A former radio station owner from Bismarck, North Dakota, Ben Neilsen understands the importance of positive self-worth. He recalls, "The thing that I didn't do originally is that I didn't really love myself." He pauses and asks, "Who was it that touched my knees one night?"

Julia, a family therapist, remembers the incident, "Me, I said I loved your bony knees."

Ben, a 6'6" former West Pointer, sits transfixed for a moment recalling every detail. A few moments pass and a tear slides down his face. He composes himself and concludes, "That was a dear time. How the hell can you love another person if you don't love yourself?"

• • •

Happily married spouses love themselves and they love each other. This love includes respect, empathy, and unconditional acceptance. It shows itself in understanding and supportive behaviors. Loving couples accept each other as they are. The language used to discuss this positive regard is referred to variously as respect, consideration, and unconditional love. Just as their expectations for the marriage are not unrealistically high, their expectations for each other are not out of sight. Not only do they accept each other, they often come to appreciate the other person's idiosyncrasies.

If people could only learn one lesson about lasting love, they would probably be best served by learning about unconditional acceptance, which is shown through understanding and support. As early as 1979, the well-known marital researchers Lewis and Spanier showed that happy and unhappy couples differ on the accuracy of their perception of each other. They maintained that spousal accuracy in sending and receiving information is necessary not only in avoiding poor communication, but in improving mutual understanding. Erich Kirchler, from the University of Linz, in Austria, explains, "Perceiving the partner's motivations accurately is a highly important prerequisite to marital harmony. Assuming a circular effect, we may conclude that being unaware or unable to perceive the other's situation accurately is likely to provoke negative conflicts and consequently marital dissatisfaction."

The person on the street agrees with the experts. *USA Today* has identified the keys to a good relationship with one's mate. Among them are being good friends (identified by 92 percent of the people polled) and providing support and encouragement (identified by 88 percent of those asked). The couples in long marriages agree. Demonstrating understanding and support are the most important factors to a long and happy marriage.

When we respect another, we show positive regard or consideration. Harriet Davis, a Mormon wife from Urbana, Illinois, explains her highly satisfying marriage. "I think general respect for one another, patience, and understanding is just what love is. It's respect and patience—allowing for differences and knowing that people are going to be different."

If someone asks her husband how they might have the same happiness, what advice would he offer? Fred Davis enumerates, "First of all, they've got to have respect for one another. Second of all, it's strictly a give-and-take situation. Sometimes it's more me taking than giving. But between the two of us, I think it's a give-and-take, it's a trade-off."

Television personality Dick Van Patten was asked in a television interview the advice he would provide to husbands who wanted satisfying marriages. His response? "Treat your wife like a guest in the house."

Katrina and Rudy Bemke, an egalitarian, childless, community-minded, Congregational couple, each of whom is seventy-four years old, feel the secret to their success is teamwork. In addition, courtesy marks their relationship. Katrina notes, "We are both very courteous to each other, always."

Empathy, the ability to view the world through another person's eyes, is more difficult to experience and demonstrate than respect. Nonetheless, contemporary researchers have shown that marital satisfaction is related to perspective taking and empathy. Some couples discuss the importance of empathy in their day-to-day interactions. Toni Rizzo, an Italian Catholic woman, married fifty years and from Toms River, New Jersey, says, "I think the most important thing is consideration for how each person feels in each situation. You've got to put yourself in that person's place. Now we may have been swamped with people [guests in their home] all of a sudden. I can handle that, and he can't. I put myself in his place, and what I will do is subtly say to the people, 'Let us know the next time. Suppose we make it next Saturday, in a week or two.' I want to give him time to recover and think about it. I would call this consideration for the other person's feelings." Family researchers would probably call this insightful.

• • •

Ben Neilsen began his college education at the University of Minnesota. During his second year of classes, he received an appointment to West Point. With confidence he "bellered out" in class, "I'm leaving Minnesota for West Point. Anybody know any girls in the New York area?" One of his classmates, a friend named Dick Jones, gave him the name of Julia Meyer, at Wellesley College. Ben knew so little geography that he incorrectly addressed the envelope to Wellesley College in Boston. Fortunately, the postmaster understood the error and delivered the letter.

Julia looks back. "My little-girl dream had been that I would date a West Pointer, visit the Naval Academy, and go to the Dartmouth Green Key. I had gone to the Naval Academy with a family friend, and the Dartmouth Green Key guy flunked out so I was out of luck there. But then I received this letter in the mail. I just went 'wheeing' around. It was terrific. I wrote back, because I'm 5'10", or was then, and I said, 'Dick, who is this man?' Dick [her good friend who set the two of them up] hadn't thought to write to say I was going to get this letter. He wrote and said Ben was a wonderful man in his fraternity. So I wrote, 'Ben, I hope you're prepared for the height question. I'm 5'10".' He wrote back and he said, 'Don't worry about height.' He never told me how tall he was." Her husband stands 6'6 1/2".

In September of 1941, the two met. Julia went to a West Point football game with two of her friends. She recalls, "I couldn't meet him until after the football game, so here I am sitting down when this man comes up with an overcoat that goes from the ankles up. I thought I'd never get to the top. No problem with height. I thought he was handsome, and it was pretty much love at first sight."

Ben summons up, "Oh, God, she was gorgeous!"

The couple had dinner together on their first date, and they enjoyed each other's company so completely that they were still talking when the restaurant closed. They both remember the evening with great fondness. They felt at ease, they had a great deal in common, and they had fun.

Their courtship began with friendship rather than with romance. Julia remembers, "We were very restricted. We couldn't even hold hands. Even though there was a strong attraction, we had to relate in other ways, which was really a great asset." The two were friends before they were lovers. They relied on their physical attraction, mutual likes, and similarities as the basis for their relationship.

One of the ways they maintained the relationship was through the mail. The two wrote about their interests, what they liked, and how they felt about things. They also disclosed their deep feelings for each other. Some of the letters were so steamy that after they were married and had children, Ben

wanted to burn them. Julia managed to rescue the letters, but she was care-
ful to keep them from their children, even after they were grown.

Julia graduated the year before Ben did. They became officially engaged
at the end of her senior year, although they were pinned the year before. West
Point rules disallowed cadets from marrying, so the two had to wait to
marry until Ben graduated. Julia got a job just across the river from where
Ben was. She frequently went down to New York City on a train, crossed the
river, and then came back up the West Point side to be with him.

• • •

Just as empathy is more difficult to demonstrate than respect, unconditional love moves a person to another higher level. Unconditional love is love without qualification. It does not allow the conditional "If you do this, then I will love you." It may be impossible for many people to achieve; nonetheless, satisfied couples in long marriages express the importance of this form of acceptance. They communicate unconditional love in a variety of ways. Although the Harrises, married seventy-one years, do not know the family communication jargon, they certainly understood the concept. Jane Harris explains, "I think the real love comes afterwards."

"The longer you're together?"

She smiles mysteriously. "The longer you're together."

Understanding may result in a sense of peacefulness in the marriage. In the Salerno home, a feeling of relaxation and calm pervades the atmosphere. Leo Salerno explains, "What's important is if you feel comfortable with the other person, and when you're with them, you get a feeling of relaxation; there's no tension. A good marriage has to be relaxed. Relaxation and a lack of tension are important. I'm talking about monetary things, sexuality, religion, friendship, association, acquaintances. The more relaxed two people are, the better chance they have for success."

Understanding allows people to be increasingly honest with each other. If you believe another person will understand, or attempt to understand your behavior, you may be more willing to express yourself. Jane Harris discusses friendship. She suggests that the understanding offered her by her friends allowed her to be honest. She describes her friendship with a woman she had known all of her life and then recalled, "Well, she knows me well. One time I told her I wouldn't visit her at her cabin. She said, 'You're not telling me why you won't come.' My husband was sitting there listening to this, and I said, 'Frankly, Miriam, I can't sleep on that bed.' Ken [her husband] said, 'I apologize for my wife. That's a very rude thing to say.' She said, 'Now listen Ken, I don't want you to interfere between Jane and me. Our friendship is based on truth. I know she cares about me, and what she says to me is never malicious. She's just telling me the truth. And that's the way I want it, so you just keep still.' So she got a new bed. Now that's what I call a real relationship. But you can't have that with most people."

Understanding is not easy to achieve. The Mutt-and-Jeff Callahans from Boston discuss understanding. Jim offers, "We do it constantly. In fact, we were talking about it last night. And I think she summed it up as well as it can be in that we both work at it, and that we want it to happen, and we make sure it does happen. We pay a lot of attention to our relationship."

People often become closer when they go through difficult times together. Couples with long and happy marriages experience traumatic times and great difficulties. They lose parents, children, and other family members. They contract serious and life-threatening illnesses. They lose important jobs, and experience maltreatment in ongoing careers. Perhaps because they are in the trenches together, they become as close as army buddies ready to fight the enemy.

Kenneth and Jane Harris have gone through Ken's several mental breakdowns. Jane reports that she had wonderful friends who demonstrated their understanding during these difficult periods. She recalls, "They knew he was gone in the hospital, and they were wonderful. And you can't forget that. Some of them are now dead, and I miss them terribly. You can't get that kind of friendship in just a few years. It's important in a marriage and in a friendship. If you go through difficult times together and you face it together, there's a kind of bonding that goes on that doesn't happen if everything is good times. You don't have that same closeness."

● ● ●

The Neilsens are unique in that they describe the "several marriages" they have each had. While they have been married for forty-seven years exclusively to each other, they maintain that they have gone through several major changes which constitute clearly different "marriages." They began as a traditional couple. Ben graduated from West Point the year after Julia graduated from Wellesley, but she put her thoughts of a career away when she wed. They had five daughters over an eleven-year span of time. When the children were in school, Julia began to think about her own life. She went to graduate school and became a family therapist. Her education and career had major impact on her personal relationship.

Julia describes her life. "I was very traditional. I grew up with the idea that the husband is the boss. Ben grew up with that, too. I was a very dutiful, housebound hausfrau and thought I was happy in it. But then when the last child went to kindergarten, I came home one day and it was just like a knife in my stomach and I thought, 'Oh, what's going on?' I was taking a class and we had to write a paper 'How My Life Is Today and How It Will Be Ten Years from Now.' That was the night I realized that there would be two kids left at home and these kids are my life and that's not what I want.

"I started taking more classes. Then I met Virginia Satir, my idol and my mentor. I took a three-day workshop with her and then the whole family went down and we had a week with her in a family workshop. And we started in then, and we talked, and we evolved. That was in my forties, my early forties. I got my degree and went to work. I never worked nine to five. I worked in a clinic for eight years and then I went completely solo. I love it. Going back to school was one of the most exciting things. I forgot I had brains, and I had gone to a good undergraduate school, so I should have known I had brains. They kind of got lost in the shuffle. When I look back, what I did took much intelligence and planning and skill, but the book-kind of learning I had set by the wayside."

Ben agrees, "She's like a different woman. You can't stay the same. When one party changes in a marriage the other party changes or it's over."

Julia recalls, "That was a crisis. Ben's initial response was not good. I was sitting on the couch and he moved toward me and I said, 'Don't crowd me,' and I realized that's what I had felt for twenty years. I had been smothered. I told him, 'I'm going out into a field, and I'm going to run in the field freely. You have to drop the leash, Ben. Now if you want to come with me, that's wonderful.' I really issued an ultimatum. I did that and for about two months, nothing more was said. Then Ben said, 'I'm going off to workshops.' He went off by himself. That's when the whole change process began. One of our kids said, 'Mom, I want you to know that now I'm proud of you.' I thought for twenty years I was being the ideal mother."

Ben adds, "She became a much more interesting woman."

Julia asserts, "It's like a whole new marriage."

Ben is honest about his feelings. "I hadn't been all that comfortable before anyway. Things like stomachaches, headaches, and other things. I knew there were things wrong that I thought I could change or I could get help to change. But when this crisis came up, it seemed like a good possibility, a new way of looking at each other."

• • •

Satisfied couples show their love in a variety of ways. For instance, Hugh and Mary Carol O'Brien, a Milton Bradley Company inventor and his wife, are not wealthy, but they retired comfortably. When Mary Carol was young, she remarked to Hugh that before she died, she would like to own a Cadillac. Almost forty years later, Hugh remembered her wish. Mary Carol is amazed at his memory. She explains, "I was very young. This was years and years ago. I said, 'Before I ride in a Cadillac hearse, I want to own my own Cadillac.' He never forgot that. So that's how he is. He bought a Cadillac and put it in my name. It's my car." More important than the Cadillac was Hugh's memory of her fantasy.

Jergen and Inga Schultz, Germans who have already celebrated their golden wedding anniversary, show their love for each other through different means. Inga is a gourmet cook and makes wonderful meals for Jergen. With the possible exception of one recent time, Jergen has never even emptied the dishwasher. On the other hand, Jergen is caring for Inga, too. She explains, "We will be out shopping, and I will just say casually, 'Oh, that's nice,' and then, of course, he goes and buys it. So I have to be very careful about what I say is nice." Jergen has something in common with Hugh O'Brien.

Understanding another person is difficult. A seminal communication book observed that communication may fail on two levels: first, when understanding is inaccurate and second, when people do not realize their messages are misunderstood. Couples, especially those in long-term marriages, may find particular difficulty in the second level since familiarity increases an individual's confidence in his or her ability to understand others. Because of the length of their relationship, couples may believe they understand their partner even when they do not.

Couples who have had long and happy marriages, as opposed to those who have simply been married for a long time, may be distinguished on the basis of their understanding. In general, people in satisfying marriages evidence high levels of understanding and seem more inclined to consistently come to the aid of their partner.

• • •

Ben Neilsen explains how understanding works in his happy marriage. "When the schedule calls for a trip or a concert, and we either get up to the time, or we get into the concert, we see what's going on with us individually. I think, 'Gee, this isn't the concert I wanted to hear,' or 'I'm dreading this trip.' She can say, 'Hey, what are you feeling about this trip?' 'My God, it doesn't sound like anything we want to do.' Then we cancel it. The arriving at that is delicate because we made a commitment, we may have made a down payment, it might be something that one person wanted more than the other, but we're able to know this and examine it. Sometimes we do things individually, not together. We'll take two cars to some events. We don't feel trapped and we don't feel like martyrs."

• • •

Support is linked to understanding, but spouses do not always provide this support to each other. Support is not a behavior that simply originates in receivers of messages without regard for the senders. Support occurs between two people; it does not reside within one person. It is based on our communication not on our individual personality. The two members of the couple and the interaction between them must all be considered.

Courtney Salerno supports Leo verbally. Leo recalls their early days together. "You know after the war years, I was working two jobs and hustling and I wondered, 'Where's the end of the line?' She'd say, 'Hang in there. Things will come around. Things will work out.'" Such comments demonstrate support of the spouse; they also reflect the positive, optimistic attitude held by the successful couples. When the events in their life were difficult, the couples believed they would improve; when things went well, they predicted they would continue to be rosy.

Support is most frequently cited when one member of the couple faces difficulty or trauma based on work or career. Walter and Laura Clausen are from Minnesota and have been married for forty-three years. Walter chose dentistry as his profession. He details, "I can give you an example of the support I had from Laura in my middle years when I was involved in my profession.

There's a conflict between a profession and a marriage. I was involved for a period of eight years with state boards and regional boards, and Laura, almost without exception, traveled with me. I was also running a practice. Most of the time the travel involved weekends—from Friday to Monday. If we were giving boards, we would go on a Monday and come back on Wednesday.

"Laura almost invariably went with me and sat in the hotel room. That's support. It was very boring for her, except that we would go out to eat. A lot of the men's wives did that, but Laura did it a lot more. She was free to go because our family was raised. They were in college at that time. She would wait in the hotel room while I went and did my job."

Rudy Bemke, from Wisconsin, had an important post in the Rotary. He felt Katrina had been instrumental in his ability to conduct his duties. He remarks, "I think support is natural with each of us. When I was nominated to become governor of the state for Rotary, I said to her, 'Do you think we can handle it?' There are a lot of guys who'd say, 'I'm gonna take the job and you tag along behind.' I said, 'Do you think you're willing to sacrifice a year of your life for this?' And she thought about it and said, 'Well, sure, if you want to do it.' We spent 300 days out of the 365 days that year on Rotary. And you know what happened to our social life— her social life. You end up giving a year of your life to it."

He goes on, "So she gave a year of her life. At the same time, I took the job as moderator of the church, which has two thousand members. Then our minister decided to resign, so here I'm governor and moderator of a church of two thousand people with all kinds of problems. I think the support she gave me to carry on these jobs was really something. And now she's a national officer. So now it's my turn to support her."

Patricia Gronbeck, also from Wisconsin, is a highly independent woman who has been married for forty-four years. She and her husband have different nationalities, political party affiliations, and beliefs. She completed her college education after she was married. She began teaching elementary school after her children were grown. She specifies that Carl allowed her to listen to her own drummer, which included postponing work until the children were out of the home. "Well, the children were young. My own mother had worked and I was alone so much. I didn't want this for our children. And Carl was supportive, even though we weren't financially flush. We weren't starving to death. We had our own house, but we could always use the money. It wasn't something he insisted on—that I go out and get a job. He never said that."

Health problems are also likely to result in support from the partner. For instance, Hugh O'Brien spent the past winter season doing all of the housework, including the ironing, when Mary Carol's arthritis was particularly bothersome. Hugh concludes, "When things are bad, you pitch in."

Carl Gronbeck observes that Patricia was especially responsive when he had problems with his teeth. He recounts, "I recently had a lot of dental work, which was very expensive. My thought was to let my teeth go—I could get dentures. I have had dental work all my life, and I thought we had spent enough of the family treasures on my teeth. Patricia said, 'You're going to get new teeth.' It's refreshing that I needed that support even though I had questions in my mind whether I needed it or not. She had no question in her mind."

Herman and Eleanor Kidd are both over eighty years old, and they have been married for fifty-seven years. Although other couples are chronologically older, the Kidds are not as active or youthful. Both have suffered from health problems. Herman reports that he had begun making all of the meals and doing all of the housework when Eleanor was recovering from hepatitis. After she recovered, he continued to make breakfast since he enjoyed it. The couple agrees that this is a positive accommodation in their relationship.

Ruth Ann Silver supports Ari during his illnesses, too. Ari stresses, "She's always been very supportive during my illnesses, more than you could ever possibly want a person to be. She never left my bedside."

Does he enjoy her attention?

His response is surprising, but showed concern for Ruth Ann. "No, I didn't. I feel that I'm going to live or die without her. It's uncomfortable for her to be there all the time. I don't want her to be so miserable. I'm concerned for her, but not for me."

Laura Clausen, the wife of the Minnesota dentist, has suffered with breast cancer. She sees support in her family coming full circle. She begins philosophically. "I think you have to be tolerant of one another's faults and I think not only of the bad things, but the good things. Sometimes the good things—a strong personality—I think it's a complete circle of tolerance for everything. Good, bad, and indifferent.

"Walt has certainly given me lots of support. It's really interesting because when I had the mastectomy, I had never been sick a day in my life. I had spent lots of time sitting by Sherry's [their daughter who had congenital problems with her kidneys] bed, let me tell you. Our other daughter had had some problems, too, and I sat by her bed, too, because Walt was busy working. But when I had the mastectomy, I really got support."

Marcia Gardener has suffered serious illness. She recalls, "I had a stroke. And he just took over—he had just retired that week—and he took over with almost everything because I couldn't do anything and that meant an awful lot. It still affects me. I can't do the work that I did before. I couldn't teach; I had to give that up. We used to spend a lot of time in our pool, and I can't do that very much anymore. I can't go shopping. We used to go shopping together, Christmas shopping and so forth, and I can't do that anymore. I can't do a lot of things, but it doesn't matter because he's always with me."

The Benediks are from Dayton, Ohio. Married forty-four years, Wayne is seventy-two and Marcia is sixty-four. Wayne was a corporation president and the couple has nine children, ranging in age from twenty-five to forty-three. Supportive behaviors have been important in raising their large family. Marcia recounts, "When there was illness in the family, you kinda pull together. In Wayne's case, his sister was very seriously ill and there was a lot of illness in his family. I think we pulled together.

"At the time of Wayne's sister's illness and death, we took it upon ourselves to adopt her daughter. So one of our nine children is an adopted child. She's the oldest, but just by six months. We didn't adopt her till she was five years old. So, maybe that was a time we—I was expecting my fourth one when we adopted Annie— we had a very bitter court battle, but I wanted the child to be raised as one of our own."

General Bradley Martin nursed his wife back to health after a nearly fatal automobile accident. He notes, "The accident called upon me to be more supportive. But Barbara is a strong character, and even without me I don't think there would've been any great problems. And our children were extremely supportive.

"At that time our son was divorced. He came and he spent about the first six weeks when she was in the hospital, and they were the worst part of it. Not only were her legs crushed, but she had peritonitis, which the doctors didn't discover for ten days. And that was the most serious thing of all because very few people survive peritonitis. That was probably the most stressful period of my life. It called upon me to be supportive and be there all the time." He adds with a smile, "Not only that, it called upon me to learn how to cook because I had never cooked in my life. And if I had before that, we would have starved to death."

Jane Harris, married seventy-one years to an inventor, discusses the support she offered during Kenneth's mental breakdowns. "It's all about caring; it's not about control. I saw what things can do to him."

She recalls with sadness, "It was very hard, but that's where I learned what friendship means. I never discussed it with my friends. I couldn't. And they never discussed it with me. But they were so wonderful." Friendship may be defined through the storms, rather than the sunny days. Further, Jane found that her supportiveness to Kenneth was rewarded with support from her friends.

• • •

Virginia Satir, the renowned family therapist, was Julia Neilsen's mentor. Both Julia and Ben loved the woman, who died just a few years ago. Ben describes Virginia, "She was just a people-lover."

Julia explains, "I think what I could say is that for the first time in my life, I had someone love me unconditionally. She loved everyone unconditionally. She was fabulous. I don't think Ben and I had ever known unconditional love. We didn't know how to accept each other. We were two kids, busy trying to change each other."

Ben agrees, "That's what we were trying to do to each other, too, conditionally loving each other."

Julia acknowledges, "I think our world has really opened up to things neither of us has known about, not grown up with. Occasionally, but not very often, do I not feel unconditional acceptance [from Ben] now. When it is, it is because he's tired or down or something, and that's okay. It's been an evolving thing."

The two describe their original families as providing conditional rather than unconditional love. Julia says, "We had to go to our room until we would come out smiling. I grew up with social pressures. Ben's family was much more restrictive. I definitely had an emotional restriction. I had a lot of freedoms, which doesn't always make sense. My dad would not let me walk to my friend's house, which was a block away, at night without him walking with me. I am not afraid of the dark, in spite of that. On the other hand, he would let me get on my bike with a peanut butter sandwich and a mason jar of water, and I could ride all day down to the river all by myself. I remember free feelings. I had a lot of moments of freedom. It was getting away from what restrictions I had. I understand now completely."

Julia shares, "I wrote to Virginia [Satir] often in the last few years. I didn't know she was ill. I had been writing to her and one of the letters was an apology. I said, 'You nurtured me all the time, but you did not ask for nurturing. I was in a place where I did not realize you needed it. Please know that I wished that I could nurture you more.' I told her how much she meant to me. I had been getting more in touch with this thing called unconditional love. I'd grown up with conditional love, and I got married with conditional love. Obviously, we loved each other. Unconditional love is a gift. Except that I'm not going to do it all the time, either. That's part of it, too. It sounds so hearts and flowers, but I know damned well I become pessimistic or judgmental. A couple needs to at least know that they're headed to unconditional love. I don't think anybody in their twenties or thirties is going to know that."

• • •

Hugh and Mary Carol O'Brien provide an example of her support for him. The interesting part of the story is that she created the problematic situation for him. Mary Carol's best friend was the wife of the company president. When she learned that the president was dating another woman and that he was divorcing his wife, Mary Carol told him what she thought of him. She added, "I don't care if you fire my husband."

While he didn't fire Hugh, he did make life very difficult at work. Shortly after this, Hugh had a heart attack. Interestingly, Mary Carol identifies her support of Hugh during this period as an example of her empathy. Mary Carol recalls, "He [Hugh] was really low. It hit his morale. He was in a corner. They hoped he would leave. I used to say, 'Hugh, never mind, just know you're loved. That's all you have to know is that you're loved.' And I know he was down because he had a heart attack right after that. It took a lot out of him." Would Hugh have similarly suffered had it not been for Mary Carol's meddling?

Hugh supports Mary Carol in a number of ways. She tends to be a conservative, fairly dependent woman. When they winter in Florida, she finds the driving to be too difficult. As a consequence, Hugh drives her everywhere. She reports, "I don't like to drive, especially here. I think it's suicide. He's taken me three times to get a cap on a tooth. A three-hour session one day and no complaints. Tuesday he took me all the way to the hematologist and sat from 1:30 until 4:00, no complaints. He does all these things, takes me to the hairdresser's. I've got a license to drive. Another husband would say, 'Drive yourself. You can drive. Drive yourself.' He takes me."

Another Irish couple adds to the conversation. Ed Delaney, an Irish comedian, becomes serious. "The other partner becomes very strong and very supportive when you've got a problem. It seems to particularly apply to women. If a man has a problem, the woman becomes very strong and supportive and can handle problems. 'I can do this and I can do this.' "

Fred Davis, the former police chief from Urbana, Illinois, had no religion when his children were at home. His wife is a devoted Mormon, but Fred never attended church when his family was growing. Harriet took the children to church each Sunday. However, Fred found a way to be supportive. "I prepared the meals on Sunday when she was gone to church 'cause normally I would go hunting or something in the morning. And I'd come home, and they'd be gone to church."

The surprising Silvers offered another revelation. Ruth Ann claims that Ari is always supportive. He quickly adds, "Although I despised her mother and father."

Ruth Ann disagrees, "No, you did not."

Ari qualifies his answer. "I didn't like your mother, for sure."

"You did not despise my father."

"Your father was barely tolerable."

Ruth Ann asserts, "He was wonderful."

Ari shoots back, "He was a very bigoted man."

Ruth Ann resumes talking about Ari, rather than her parents. "He was wonderful to my parents and he was wonderful to me."

Ari will not be silenced. "He was a terrible bigot. When Cosby appeared on TV, he turned off the TV."

Ruth Ann explains, "My father was brought up in a different era. He had different experiences."

Ari argues, "It was still bigotry."

Ruth Ann continues, "I'm not going to defend him, but my father was, in many respects, a very wonderful man. They adored each other. When my father was ill, in the later years of his life, Ari was wonderful to him. Not just to me, but to him."

"Only because of you."

Ruth Ann rests her case. "The fact remains that your behavior toward my father was far more than I could expect."

Ari tries another tack. "He never picked up a check."

Ruth Ann agrees, "He was very proud of that."

Ari remains astounded. "Can you believe that?"

Ruth Ann recalls, "He used to say to his friends, 'In all the years we have been dining out, I have never picked up a check.' "

Ari quips, "I thought he would have been ashamed."

Ruth Ann reminisces, "After my mother's funeral, he took us out for coffee. The waiter came with the check and he pointed to Ari. In his grief, he still wouldn't pay." She adds, "In many respects, Ari is a wonderful, wonderful man."

When couples engage in support, they need not become doormats for unacceptable or hurtful behavior. Family therapist Sven Wahlroos encourages family members to accept the feelings of others and to try to understand them, but not to accept all actions. Using the example of parents and children, he explains,

> Children often complain that their parents don't understand them. When you question these children a little more closely, it often turns out that they simply demand that their parents let them do whatever they want. A prohibition is interpreted by these children as a lack of "understanding." And then both parents and children, instead of differentiating between understanding feelings and accepting actions, begin to hide behind the current universal excuse for poor or destructive communication called "generation gap."

Some of the satisfied couples could not accept the behaviors of their spouse. The Silvers discussed Ruth Ann's face-lift and Ari's disagreement with the surgery. Ruth Ann begins, "When he came to visit me in the hospital before the surgery, before I was prepped, he wouldn't stay. He ran in and ran out."

"I didn't want her to do it," Ari says. "How could I support her?"

Ruth Ann sees, in retrospect, "All of the arrangements were made and we had driven into New York together—we lived in the suburbs. He dropped me, and I was to take the subway to get to the doctor. I walked to the subway, and then I came back, and I said, 'Should I do it?' He said, 'Look, you're a big girl. Make your own decisions. Stop bothering me.' And I was very hurt. I realize now that was the wisest and the best way of handling it."

The Silver's behavior demonstrates that support is not always present nor does it have to be for a marriage to be successful and long lasting. Nonetheless, attempting to understand one's partner and demonstrating that understanding result in high satisfaction. Through identification and empathy, marriage partners come to define themselves as a unit. Building such a partnership is not possible without understanding and support.

Dudley D. Cahn, who teaches at a state university in New York, explains this process. He defines perceived understanding as "an individual's assessment of his or her success when attempting to communicate." Cahn asserts that "to the extent that one feels understood, one tends to undertake or continue to interact based on the belief that he or she has tapped into the appropriate set of rules governing human interaction for that kind of situation." He notes, "A key proposition in the theory is that, as relationships mature, perceived understanding becomes more important relative to other variables."

Cahn's theorizing appears accurate as his research has shown that happily married people feel significantly more understood by their partner than unhappily married people. Interviews with divorced people revealed that their former spouses failed to understand them. Cahn concludes, "People who feel understood trust each other more." His work suggests that people make an increased effort to pay more attention to perceived understanding earlier in a developing relationship because of its importance later.

Couples mature as they become increasingly sensitive to each other's views. Maturing couples continue to integrate and reintegrate each person's view into a common set of understandings and conceptions. Less healthy, less adaptive, or less satisfied couples fail to reconcile the varying perceptions each holds.

Bill Cosby considers long-term marriages and how couples come to understand and accept each other.

> I will never forget my first awareness that my mother and father had ascended to a matrimonial plane where only God knew what they were doing—perhaps. We were driving to Philadelphia from Atlantic City, with my father at the wheel, my mother beside him, and me in the back.

"Oh, there's a car from Pittsburgh," said my mother, looking at a license plate in the next lane.

"How do you know it's from Pittsburgh?" said my father.

"Because I couldn't think of Pennsylvania," she replied.

And I waited for my father to respond to this Einsteinian leap into another dimension, but he didn't speak. He simply continued to drive, a supremely contented man. . . . He had understood that my mother's Pittsburgh was a mythical place, located where the Monongahela entered the twilight zone.

• • •

Would the Neilsens prescribe their secret of unconditional love to other couples? Ben hesitates, "I don't necessarily think this is the way to do it. I'm kind of suspicious of people who are up there on the stump saying, 'Look at how I made my marriage work.' "

Julia shares, "We saw a couple yesterday, and I felt so sad for them. They were constantly criticizing each other when they talked. Life is too short. When I became a family therapist and had been for four or five years, people would say, 'Oh, you have the perfect marriage.' And the kids really got it, too: 'Oh, your mother is a family therapist.' We recognized that kind of fishbowl stuff—we hadn't anticipated that. People would suddenly look to us as a model. They were sometimes sarcastic or kidding. It was a needling type thing. We felt more on display than we ever had. We told the kids not to worry about it."

• • •

Although the Neilsens do not wish to be a model for others, they clearly are. They are very loving and accepting of each other. They are autonomous, separate beings who have learned to live peaceably side by side. Their sex life is enviable. Their experiences are rich with meaning. We will hear their voices and the voices of the other couples in upcoming chapters as we explore people actively engaged in creating happy, long-term marriages. In the next chapter the role of positiveness is explored, and you will meet the Gardeners, who stand in strong contrast to the Neilsens.

Chapter 5

Positive Distortion: "The Most Beautiful Woman in the World"

Love is the magician, the enchanter, that changes worthless things to joy, and makes right royal kings and queens of common clay.

—Robert G. Ingersoll

Gus Gardener washes on his hands and knees the linoleum floor of the home he and Marcia share. He is comfortable talking to strangers from this position. Marcia sits at the kitchen table. Family pictures of themselves, their three children, and multiple grandchildren are everywhere. None of their children—born in 1946, 1948, and 1950—have divorced.

Both Gus and Marcia are of good height; she is nearly 5'9" and he is 6'. Their slenderness makes them appear taller. Marcia has suffered a stroke, and the signs are visible to a visitor. One side of her face and body is largely immobile. Partly because of the paralysis and partly because of her wrinkled and loose skin, Marcia looks her age. She dresses in multicolored, loose-fitting cotton housedresses and cardigan sweaters. Gus wears glasses and dresses in dark gray work pants and boots. He commonly wears old, stretched-out white T-shirts. Married forty-eight years, they have lived most of their life in Wisconsin, where he was a mail carrier and she was an elementary schoolteacher. Gus graduated from high school while Marcia finished her college degree after all of their children were educated.

Why did Gus and Marcia marry? With love in his heart and a glow in his eyes, Gus looks through rose-colored glasses at his aged, disfigured, less than ordinary-looking wife and asks, "Are you kidding? Look at her." Then he makes a serious, passionate pronouncement. "She's the most beautiful woman in the world."

• • •

Three brilliant individuals were discussing the greatest contribution or invention of all time. The first person was a journalist and he said the greatest development was the newspaper. Every morning and every evening you could learn about everything that had occurred in the world that day. Almost like magic you were presented with all of the information you could ever want.

The second person, who was in the media, disagreed. She said the greatest invention was the television. Not only did it provide all of the information about the world's happenings, but the information was provided both orally and visually. The television informed you and it entertained you.

The third person was unemployed, but he disagreed with the first two. He said the newspaper was useful and the television was entertaining, but the most impressive development of all times was the thermos bottle. The other two acted surprised and they asked the third person why he felt the thermos bottle was such an impressive invention. "Well," he said, "It keeps hot things hot and cold things cold." "Yes," said the other two, "so?" "Well," said the third man, "how does it know?"

When Whitney Houston asked, "How will I know?" in her popular song in the late 1980s, she was inquiring about how a person knows if their partner is the "right one." We have no entrance exams, no standardized tests, no previous scores to use to determine if someone should be our partner for life. We similarly have no way of knowing if the behavior we exhibit and the behavior our spouse exhibits is "correct" or useful or appropriate. Each of us has our own experience with marriage and we are free to define our partners and our marriage as we will.

An educator tried to distinguish between objective, subjective, and existentialist views of reality by using a baseball metaphor. The professor noted, "Objective reality is when you state that a ball is a ball and a strike is a strike and umpires call them as they are. Subjective reality is when a ball is a ball and a strike is a strike but umpires call them as they see them. Existentialist reality is when umpires state that a ball is not a ball and a strike is not a strike until they call them."

We might guess that couples who have a realistic (or objectively verified) view of each other and each other's behavior are more satisfied than those who hold distorted (subjective or existentialist) views. Just the opposite is true. Couples who positively distort their partner's communicative behavior are more satisfied with their marriage than couples who do not distort their partner's behavior. In other words, to the extent couples perceive their partner's behavior uniquely and favorably, they also are more favorably disposed in rating their marital satisfaction.

Happy couples have an internal locus of evaluation. They do not view the world nor their marriage through objective eyes. Many of their lives and marriages appear ordinary or pedestrian to an outsider, but the couple see themselves as extraordinary. Happy couples do not take their cues from the rest of the world. They determine their own reality. Perhaps they are happy because they believe they are happy. They appear to universally distort, in a positive way, the experiences and behaviors they share. Indeed, Clyde and Susan Hendrick, from Texas Tech University, showed that people in love view the world differently from people not in love. They concluded that "lovers wear rose-colored glasses." Love may not be "blind," but it does evidence some astigmatism.

Virtually all satisfied couples, for example, state that they are open and honest with each other, even though the actual levels of openness and honesty vary dramatically from one couple to the next. Some would have judged them to be low in disclosure, but they feel they "talk about everything." They perceive their marriage to include a lot of talk and, more specifically, self-talk. Happy couples do not necessarily tell their spouses everything. For some, secrets are necessary. In spite of this, they go right on believing that they "tell all."

When the couples are asked directly if they share all or most of their experiences with their partner, they are unanimous in agreement. I asked some of the couples who had earlier stated that they disclose everything, "Have you talked about what would happen if one of you would die?"

"Well, no."

"Since only one of you takes care of all of the investments and the bills, have you discussed your financial situation with your spouse?"

"I don't really understand all of that."

"Do you talk about your sex life?"

"That's not appropriate."

"Do you share problems?"

"He doesn't like to hear negative things."

Couples may feel it is socially desirable to state that they share all information, even though they do not. Earlier research suggesting satisfied couples self-disclose completely was based on self-report information. The couples in this study, too, reported that they shared all. The finding that they do not is only revealed through additional probes and more indirect questions.

Similarly, to a couple, the happy couples declare that they rarely have conflict. Observers outside the relationship may categorize their communicative behavior as filled with bickering, as in the case of the Silvers, but the couple perceive that they get along well and rarely have a disagreement. Other couples seem to disagree, too, but they do not identify the communication as conflict. Marital researchers MacKinnon, MacKinnon, and Franken found that people in strong, long-term marriages redefined stressful and conflictual events to make them more manageable. They held idealistic attitudes about the probability of relationship conflicts and were confident of their successful resolution.

Every marriage has conflicts and problems, but more satisfied couples define them differently than people in unhappy relationships. Fincham and Bradbury, two researchers, showed that the quality of one's marriage is positively related to one's attributional styles. People in happier relationships blame outside forces or unusual circumstances, not their spouse. They express the sentiment that their spouse is motivated by good intentions and that difficulties he or she has created are unintended, not worthy of blame, and not selfishly motivated.

Part of what occurs in long-term, happy marriages is that partners learn, in Kenny Rogers's words, "when to hold them and when to fold them." They may choose their battles carefully and be willing to forgive and forget a number of everyday occurrences. Larry L. Constantine, the editor of a special issue of *Lifestyle* on long-term marriages, and on the faculty of Family Studies at the

University of Connecticut, in Storrs, provides a delightful description of one of the factors leading to a happy, long-term marriage:

> There is something else to our durability as a couple, although I often forget what it is. Oh yes, *forgetfulness*. As the relationship survives, as it enriches and broadens, but especially as the old gray matter begins to wear thin, one forgets what some of the earlier struggles were about. Maybe it really didn't matter and maybe it did, but I can't remember what we were fighting about or why it seemed so outrageously and ultimately important. The early tendrils of senility can do wonders to help keep the focus on the here-and-now. You can't keep fighting about the same things when you can't remember the problem. Of course, there are still things we have to work out, in fact, there are a couple of things I have been meaning to take up with Joan, but, oh well, I can't think of them at the moment.

Not only do the happily wed have subjective or even existentialist views of their marriage, they also come to share this view with each other. One explanation for this common view comes from a theory known as symbolic interactionism. This theory suggests that when people interact with each other over time, they begin to develop and maintain a common way of viewing events. Repeated interactions allow greater opportunities for shared perspectives. Since couples in long-term marriages have a longer period of interaction, they become highly similar in their relative perceptions.

People vary from each other in how they view the world, and they tend to maintain their unique perspective. This notion is illustrated in the story told about a college student in a large lecture class. This particular student was taking a true-false exam, and he sat in the back of the room flipping a coin while he took the exam. He would flip the coin, write down an answer, flip the coin, mark an answer, and so on. Toward the end of the period, the professor noticed that he was flipping the coin in rapid succession while he glanced at his exam. The professor was curious about what he was doing and walked to the back of the room and asked him. The student responded that he had ten minutes left so he was checking his answers.

This story illustrates that people have different ways of viewing the world and that they generally view it consistently. If a person has particular biases, he or she will seek out examples that demonstrate or confirm the bias. Even in the presence of counterexamples, an individual will cling to his or her beliefs. Happily married couples follow the same principle.

In countless ways, satisfied couples maintain one set of behaviors but demonstrate, in their interactions, totally different actions. Should we conclude that happy couples have a poor grip on reality? Perhaps they do, but is the reality of one's marriage better known by outside onlookers than by the players themselves? The conclusion is evident. One key to a long happy marriage is to tell yourself and others that you have one and then to behave as though you do!

• • •

Gus and Marcia Gardener recall their first meeting vividly. Marcia was enrolled in a teacher's training class and the school scheduled a dance in which the women were to invite the men. She invited someone else, but one of her friends invited Gus. The two couples went out to another dance after the school dance had ended. Although they were with other people, the two fell in love that night. They went with no one else after that time nearly fifty years ago. Gus and Marcia were drawn together because of similarity: they were both tall, they had similar personalities, they loved to dance, and they had great senses of humor.

Their first date was a boat trip across Lake Michigan. Marcia hesitated when Gus asked her because her mother owned a restaurant and she was on vacation. She depended on Marcia to run the business. Marcia was strongly attracted to Gus, however, and she managed to convince her aunt to work for her. Gus picked her up at quarter to five in the morning and they didn't get back until six-thirty the next morning. Marcia recalls, "That was quite a date." She admits that if her mother had been at home she might not have been able to be gone for over twenty-four hours with her new beau.

• • •

People who view events more favorably consistently view both their partner's communicative behavior and their marital satisfaction more favorably. Indeed, long-term happily married couples

76

view their partner, their marriage, and other events as highly positive. Even in the face of difficult times, health problems, death, and other disasters, these couples maintain their "Pollyanna" outlook.

Couples in happy marriages put a positive interpretation on many events. For instance, a recent study found that women who have positive relationships with their mother do better in their own marriage than those who do not. Another study showed that when dating couples are positive in their premarital relationship, they are more likely to be satisfied within their marriage. Satisfied spouses tend to view most of their relationships as positive and they attempt to interact with others in a positive way.

The happily wed are not simply happy about their marriage: they are often happy in general. They put a positive patina on what might appear to be a fairly ordinary existence. These folks have taken, literally, the words of a song—"Don't worry—be happy." Their positiveness includes a sense of certainty, acceptance, affirmation. Their marriage has a forward motion to it, and they sense that they are making progress and moving ahead. They admit of little doubt. Happy couples de-emphasize the negative and emphasize the positive.

The Silvers, from New York, bicker in every interaction, but they still view each other very positively. Ruth Ann claims, "In many respects, Ari is a wonderful, wonderful man."

Ari adds, "I've always admired her and respected her."

Recognizing that they are behaving out of character, Ruth Ann cracks, "We sound like Mr. and Mrs. Pollyanna."

Ari becomes serious. "It's a terrible thing, but I know that she's a lot smarter than me in many ways on many things."

"Yes, I chose well," Ruth Ann says. She asks her husband, "So tell me, Mr. Silver, why have you stayed married to me all these years?"

"Because you're a hot, sexy number," Ari says.

The long-term happily wed understand intuitively the concept of the self-fulfilling prophecy. This idea suggests that if we treat people a certain way, then they will become more like the way we treat them. If you treat a child as though he or she is exceptionally bright, he or she will actually perform better in academic work. Similarly, if you treat another person as though they are worthy of love, they will behave in a consistent manner.

Toni Rizzo illustrates the self-fulfilling prophecy. "There's good in everybody. Even if a person doesn't know there's good in them you can get it out eventually. You act in certain ways and you're good to each other and pretty soon you'll feel that kind of love and affection. I do that with my granddaughter. People think she is the biggest brat, but I constantly tell her what a good kid she is and then she behaves that way. My daughter goes, 'Ma, how do you accomplish these things?' I said, 'I don't know, I just want them to be good.' The younger one gave both her mother and father, who are separated, a bad time. One morning at breakfast she said something like, 'They make me feel like I'm a problem child.' So I said, 'Don't you dare use that word in connection with your name. Don't ever think it, don't ever feel it, don't let anyone think it, or say it.' I said, 'And I'm warning you now, I never want to hear it again.' Well, her face brightened up and she turned to her girlfriend and said, 'See, I am good, you know.' And I saw it and I called my daughter and I said, 'She was marvelous,' and she said, 'Ma, I don't know how you accomplish this.'"

Cookie Simonian tells a similar story. "The day after we got engaged, Sam was driving a delivery truck for his cleaning place, and I went with him. Sam went into a customer's house, and he came out, and he told the woman he had just gotten engaged the night before. The woman said, 'Sam, I have to give you one piece of advice: tell your wife every day of your married life that you love her.' Both of us tell each other, I don't know how many times, during every day. Also, if he does something good, I compliment him. If I do something good, he compliments me. For instance, he brags about my cooking in front of me." Erich Kirchler, from the University of Linz, Austria, would probably encourage such behavior since he found that marital happiness is associated with such positivity.

• • •

The Gardeners began their marriage with an unconventional wedding. Marcia explains, "I married on my twenty-first birthday. That was pretty young. I broke my foot the day of the wedding. I had forgotten that I needed some mint and nut cups on the tables for the reception. We lived upstairs, Mother and I. I was running down the steps to get the mint and nut cups—I always ran two at a time—I landed with my ankle turned and fell and broke it. That was the day of the wedding. It was swollen and numb,

78

and I walked down the aisle on a broken foot. It ended up in the paper,
'She would have walked down the aisle if her foot would have been broken
off.'"

Gus smiles, *"I went through the bridal dance with her mother because*
she couldn't do it."

• • •

In general, the happy couples are optimistic. One observer noted that the difference between an optimist and a pessimist was that the optimist believes this is the best possible world and the pessimist knows that it is. The long-term happily marrieds exhibit their exuberance from believing that they have helped to create the best possible worlds for themselves and their mate.

Not only are happy couples likely to interpret their experiences as positive, they are also more likely to engage in positive behaviors. What are positive behaviors? They include a voice filled with caring, warmth, tenderness, empathy, cheerfulness, affection, buoyancy, concern, and laughter. Satisfied spouses agree more often. They are more likely to positively reinforce each other. They tend to confirm the messages offered by their spouse. They are more likely to exchange smiles, hugs, and compliments. They offer both unconditional positive behaviors, which are for being, including smiling, hugging, saying "I love you," or "You look terrific," and conditional ones, which are for doing, such as "Thanks for the backrub," "Your dinner was delicious," "I appreciate your picking up my shirts," and "You did a good job of cleaning the garage." A spiraling positive effect emerges. More satisfied couples use more frequent, positive, and effective interaction, which leads to greater satisfaction.

Humor is an important strategy to maintain positiveness, especially in light of all of the unexpected crises that occur in families. Ed Delaney, an Irish storyteller from Chicago, shares, "I think one of the most important things is that you both have a sense of humor, a real genuine sense of humor."

He reflects on his sister, whose husband has no sense of humor. "It's sad. My sister is not very happy, but she is determined that the marriage will work because the alternative is that she would have to be alone. She wants some companionship. Her life could be so much better. Humor can overcome all kinds of adversity."

Gina Daley, an Italian woman married to another Irishman, agrees. "I think you should have a good sense of humor, both parties should have a good sense of humor." She recalls a story about her grandson to illustrate that their family has well-developed senses of humor. "He's seventeen now, but when he was about two or three, I got after him for something. I can't remember what it was, so he goes running to Grandpa and he says, 'Grandpa, you can take your Grandma and go home.'"

Rudy Bemke, too, recalls, "When we were first married, we lived on this meager salary, and she always kidded. She'd say, 'We have 50 cents left. Which of us goes to the movies?' Rather than me saying 'What the hell are we going to do?' We'd kid about it. 'We have 50 cents left.'"

Jackie Stanowski similarly advises, "Laugh a lot. Find humor in all the dumb things that you do." She recounts the previous week, when friends visited them but were reluctant to eat anything in their home. After they were gone, she realized that everything was either from a health store, was low in calories, had no sugar, or was reduced in fat. She laughs and wonders if they had gone back to a normal diet after visiting them.

• • •

The Gardeners owned a restaurant in Sturgeon Bay, Wisconsin, during part of their marriage. On a very hot Sunday afternoon, some of their relatives came to visit from the nearby town of Algoona, which was much cooler than Sturgeon Bay. The relatives invited Gus, Marcia, and their children back to their home to cool off after they closed the restaurant. The couple agreed and took off with the two of them, Marcia's mother, and their three children. The two girls were in the front seat with Marcia, and they fell asleep so they were left in the car.

When the family was ready to leave, Gus asked Marcia to drive since he had a headache. She agreed and got in the driver's seat, and the girls were still sleeping in the seat next to her. Marcia's mother squeezed in the front seat, too, to help with the little girls. Gus carried his now-sleeping son to the car and told the two women that he would put him in the back seat with him. He put the boy in the car and slammed the door shut and, bam, Marcia gunned the engine and took off. She had a heavy foot and they made good progress. On the way back to Sturgeon Bay, they passed through a tiny town in which Gus had a cousin who owned the only tavern. Marcia was surprised to see that Arnie's tavern was locked up already, since it was well before the legal time to stop serving alcohol in Wisconsin. She said to Gus, "Look, Arnie's all locked up already." Gus didn't answer and Marcia concluded that he was sleeping. Her mother, half drowsy, raised up, but without looking back, replied, "Oh, he's asleep."

Later Marcia asked Gus for his billfold because the car was out of gas. She was afraid they would end up walking if they didn't find a station. Finally they found a filling station and Marcia pulled next to the pumps. She turned around in the car, but she couldn't see Gus. Upset, she told her mother, "He's not in that back seat."

Her mother was more easygoing. "He has to be. A grown up man doesn't fall out of the car."

Marcia realized that she had left Gus back with her relatives. He had put their son in the car, but he hadn't gotten in. Instead, he had walked around to the other side, but before he could get in, Marcia had driven off. It was midnight or after when she left the relatives, it was dark, and she couldn't see. As a fast driver, Marcia didn't waste any time. A group of relatives put Gus in another car and tried to catch up with her so they could pass her so Gus could be found hitchhiking on the road. Failing in that tack, they brought Gus to the gas station where Marcia had stopped. Everyone had a good laugh and the story ended up on the front page of the Milwaukee Journal.

• • •

Satisfied couples have positive interpretations of current events, and they also recall their earlier days together warmly. Most happily married couples can remember, in detail, the first time they met, including the clothing of their mate-to-be. Some believed they fell in love at first sight. Polish, polka-loving George Stanowski fell immediately in love with his wife, Jackie, because, in his words, "I admired her body." "Love" at first sight is probably a misnomer. Actually, many couples experience an emotional or physiological reaction to their partner within the first few moments of meeting, but it is maybe more akin to lust than to lasting, romantic love. Nonetheless, many couples married forty years or more describe the passion, excitement, or interest they felt almost immediately upon meeting their future spouse. They explain their interest by recalling their partner's looks, personality, or other characteristics.

Jim and Susie Callahan provide an example. Susie is barely five feet tall; Jim is nearly 6'6". Irish Catholics from Boston are not unusual; Jim and Susie Callahan are special. The Callahans are fun-loving and exude warmth and love. Jim is a joker, and Susie loves every minute of it. She remembers the first time they met. "We met on a blind date. He was in the navy, and I knew someone that was on the ship that he was on. And they were coming home, but the other guy didn't come home. So he called me. And then we talked, and he asked me out, so I went out. Nine days and we knew that was it. We had nine days before he had to go back."

Jim clarifies, "We had nine days before she knew it. I knew as soon as I saw her. I knew I was going to marry her as soon as I saw her walking down the stairs. I said, 'WO-OW-W! I didn't know Bo Derek lives here!' It was the first time I felt that way." Although Jim was reminded that Bo Derek had not even been born when he met Susie, he is still confident that that was what he said.

Susie adds, "And he was all of nineteen—three days short of being twenty." What attracted Susie to Jim? "Physical attractiveness," she says. "He was very romantic and very funny. He didn't tell lies—he exaggerated terrible, but they were funny things—he still does that." The Callahans are happy, past, present, and future.

Long-term happily married couples disdain negative behavior. What advice does Laura Clausen, the wife of a Minnesota dentist, have for a young couple? She responds quickly, "Be tolerant, kind, and understanding. Don't carry a grudge forever. If there was something you didn't like, forget it! Forget it and don't go back. You know some people harp on the same things—you did this to me in 1928, I remember the time. Ten, twenty, thirty years later, they're still saying that. We have never done that. Don't do that to one another. It destroys you. It destroys your relationship."

What are negative behaviors in a marriage? They include voices that are tense, whining, furious, cold, impatient, blaming, sarcastic, angry, hurt, or depressed. Happy couples avoid such non-verbal signs of negativity, and they are less likely to engage in criticism, name calling, complaining, dirty looks, and sarcastic comments than the unhappily married. As early as 1938, a study by Lewis Terman showed that unhappy couples are distinguished from happy ones by the extent to which they report their partner being argumentative, critical, nagging, and otherwise negative.

Researchers like John Gottman, at the University of Washington, have shown that unhappily married spouses show more negative emotions and they mutually exchange these negative emotions more than the happily married. Negativity and negative communication are related to relational dissatisfaction. Indeed, negative expressions in a relationship are a litmus test for discovering unhappy partners. Decreasing negative behaviors can increase couples' marital happiness.

Just as positive behaviors spiral into satisfied spouses who then use an increasing number of positive behaviors, negative behaviors also spiral. This spiraling effect seems to be particularly true in conflict. Gottman concluded that the most dysfunctional pattern, and the one most frequently enacted by unhappily married couples, is cross-complaining, a complaint-countercomplaint sequence. Another negative pattern, discovered by researcher Thomas, is the complaint-disagreement sequence.

Not only do unhappy couples use negative words and actions more often, they are also less likely to understand each other than happy couples; in fact, they appear to have a negative bias toward the messages sent by their partner. Regardless of the intent of the speaker, spouses in distressed marriages tend to evaluate the messages from their partner more negatively than spouses in satisfying marriages.

The bad news is that negative behaviors and negative perceptions wreak havoc with a happy marriage. The good news is that most couples learn to avoid negative sentiment as their marriage develops. Two researchers determined that there is significantly less negative sentiment in the marriages of older people when compared to those married for shorter periods of time. People in satisfying marriages may learn the lesson of avoiding negative behaviors and bias earlier than their dissatisfied counterparts.

• • •

The Gardeners have lived by the philosophy that you should cry when someone is born and laugh when they die. At least they have laughed in the face of death. When their entire clan would gather for a family funeral, they would celebrate the fellowship they shared. Marcia explains, "When we go to funerals, the whole relation would get together. I had seventy-five cousins. We had a big family, a lot of laughing, and at funerals, we had a good time, too. We had a very good time. It sounds odd, I think of some of the things I did at funerals. I went to my uncle's funeral and it was icy and I had just had surgery on my back so the doctor told me 'All right, you go, but be careful.' Well, I slipped and slid under the car. And I was under the car and everybody was afraid the car was going to take off, and I laid under there and laughed. I couldn't move. The whole procession was held up because I was under the car."

Marcia is thoughtful. "That might be why we have a good marriage. We saw the humor in things and were able to laugh at it instead of getting mad or upset or angry. That's the truth. We laughed at everything. It might be a good way to deal with things—it eases tension."

• • •

Just as positive words and actions lead to happiness and happiness encourages more positive behaviors, positiveness also seems to lead to other pleasant outcomes. The long-term happily married couples frequently look far younger than their years. Married forty-two years, Jackie Stanowski turned sixty-two in 1991, the same year that "Jackie O" showed us how good sixty-two could look. Jackie S., like her same-aged counterpart, looks no more than thirty-five. She is 5'3" and weighs little more than one hundred pounds. Her figure is youthful, her clothes are stylish, her hair is dark, her face is relatively unlined, except for beautiful laugh lines around her eyes and mouth. What is her secret? Activity. She became a long-distance runner at age forty-nine. She plays tennis and golf. She rides a bike and loves to walk. She and her husband go dancing at least once a week. She doesn't smoke, drinks in moderation, and is very careful about the food she eats. Her health is excellent. She looks the way every woman who is sixty-two would like to look. Her mother is ninety-nine years old.

Although we have no proof, the positive attitudes expressed by the satisfied couples may show itself in physical and psychological health. Hans J. Eysenck, Ph.D., D.Sc., is a professor at the Institute of Psychiatry at the University of London and is one of the world's most cited psychologists. He has provided evidence that some personalities are more disease-prone than others. Cancer, for instance, is related to an inability to express anxiety, fear, and anger and an inability to cope with stress as well as a tendency to have feelings of helplessness, hopelessness, and depression. He believes that body and mind are on a continuum.

Similarly, happily married couples appear to be generally physically healthy. While physical health and marital health may be related, one does not necessarily predict the other. Nonetheless, positive attitudes toward one's spouse and marriage may be related to a general positive outlook and increased physical health. Indeed, marriage itself leads to positive outcomes. A number of studies have shown that married people, regardless of satisfaction levels, report greater happiness, life satisfaction, and positive affect. One investigator concludes, "Marital status is one of the strongest single predictors of subjective well-being." This finding appears to have an even stronger effect for happy couples.

Happily married couples do not rely on others for their interpretations of their marriage. They are the architects for their well-built homes. Their marriages are marked by positiveness, frequently shown in humor, and an avoidance of negative perceptions and behaviors. In the next chapter you will meet Leonard and Darlene Dahlquist, who will illustrate that sometimes you must remain two to become one in a long-term happy marriage.

Chapter 6

Remaining Two: "I'm Just the Opposite"

It's co-existence or no-existence.

—Bertrand Russell

The Dahlquists present a distinctive view of happy marital life. They have been married forty-two years, and Darlene is sixty-nine while Leonard is seventy-three. They are Polish Catholics from Buffalo, New York. They have three grown children, but have lost one baby. Both have undergone heart attacks and bypass surgery.

Darlene has short blonde hair, glasses, an underbite, and smokes cigarettes constantly. She dresses casually in matching cotton front-button blouses and pants. She wears sandals, and she slips them off easily as she talks. She is opinionated and assertive, but also relaxed and informal.

Leonard is round, has dominant brown eyes, a perpetual smile, and gray hair. He dresses in sporty outfits, which include light blue shirts, light blue plaid pants, a yellow sports sweater, and slip-on shoes. He is not as causally dressed as his wife.

While the two are similar in some respects, there are some important differences. Darlene is angular and slender. She is highly organized and a perfectionist. She loves to talk and to take charge. In many ways, she exhibits masculine characteristics—she is ambitious, assertive, and a decision maker for the two. She is the one who decided she would like to discuss their marriage with me. She explains, "I like to do challenging things."

• • •

People who get married become one, but they also need to maintain their own identity. The importance of independence is summed up by one woman interviewed by *USA Today*. She has enjoyed a highly successful twenty-three year marriage and states she wants her four children, ranging in age from thirteen to twenty, to learn about autonomy from their parent's marriage. She explains, "I hope they've picked up that marriage is a most important commitment, but not suffocating." Couples find their way to a space between commitment and suffocation.

Researchers Schwartz and Jackson identify "being equal partners who respect each other's needs" as one element of a model marriage. Robbyn Turner and I similarly report that individuality and letting the other person be an individual are keys to success. Do couples in long-term happy marriages require autonomy?

To understand autonomy among couples, we review two models of satisfying marriages. Olson and McCubbin, two well-known family researchers, believe happy marriages include cohesion, adaptability, and communication. They define family cohesion as "the emotional bonding that family members have toward one another." Couples may be highly separate, highly intimate, or somewhere in between.

Olson and McCubbin assert that satisfied families probably lie in the midrange of cohesion.

> When cohesion levels are high (enmeshed systems), there is over-identification so that loyalty to and consensus within the family prevent individuation of family members. At the other extremes (disengaged systems), high levels of autonomy are encouraged and family members "do their own thing," with limited attachment or commitment to their family.

More recently, a communication researcher has shown that satisfied couples may fit into any of the categories of cohesion. Mary Anne Fitzpatrick, from the University of Wisconsin, Madison, identifies three types of couples. She labels these the independents, the separates, and the traditionals. Fitzpatrick's couples can be distinguished on the basis of their relative needs for independence and interdependence. For instance, the independent couples desire great autonomy, but negotiate the amount of sharing that occurs. The separate couples experience little togetherness and engage in little sharing. The traditional couples, by contrast, are represented by high interdependence and low autonomy.

In general, the individuals who comprise couples married forty years or more have less need to be self-governing than some of the literature suggests. Although some people in younger marriages, or newer marriages, may feel strong needs to govern themselves, individuals in long-term marriages exhibit few autonomy needs. In general, they have moderate to high levels of cohesion. Most long-term happily married couples represent Fitzpatrick's traditional couples, who exhibit high interdependence and low autonomy, while a few are independent couples who establish greater autonomy.

• • •

The Dahlquists have both experienced heart attacks and have lived long lives, but their first meeting at a dance made them seem like teenagers. Leonard Dahlquist slowly weaves his yarn. "It was very simple. It was after war. We were at a social. I had a date, and she had a date, but before the night was over, I went home with her, and my date went home with her date. From that day on we just—that was it—man, it was just— it's happened now. When we got married, I was thirty years old so I was pretty well settled. I had just come out of the service. I spent almost five years in the Coast Guard during the war and I figured, 'Well, I think it's about time I settled down.' The timing was perfect. We were at this party and we knew everybody, everybody knew everybody. You know it just hit like lightning."

Darlene felt the same "love at first sight" phenomenon. "Talk about love at first sight, if that's what love at first sight is, that's what it was. We kept dancing together; that's when the other two decided that we were to be together and they'd be together. My date came to me and said, 'If you like him so much, then he can take you home.' I was delighted, he was pleased. So I said to him, 'You better take care of your date.' He went to my date and said, 'Would you take her home?' And he said, 'Gladly.' In our later years my date lived within a block of us in the summers. He had married somebody entirely different, of course." *She considers her own first meeting again.* "It was cute, it was darling, and like he said, after the war we were *all ready to settle down because we had been waiting a long time. I was twenty-six: I'm four years younger. We met in the summer, we were engaged in November, and we were married June first. Less than a year."*

• • •

Many couples, unlike the Dahlquists, do not desire autonomy. Do satisfied spouses in long-term marriages need time alone for their own activities? Former inventor Hugh O'Brien responds thoughtfully, "I don't know. I don't think so. I don't feel comfortable without her, and she doesn't feel comfortable without me. She doesn't have many girlfriends and I don't have any men friends I go out and play poker with once a week."

Mary Carol O'Brien reveals that she and Hugh spend virtually every minute together. "We start out the day by going to daily Mass. Then after that we go swimming or play golf." Although like some other couples, they did volunteer work, they also did that together. Similarly, they do their shopping together, and Hugh even drives Mary Carol to her doctor or dentist appointments.

Alexander and Peggy Smith, a Baptist couple from Glen Ellyn, Illinois, are asked if they are two separate identities or one person. Alexander responds quickly, "More like one."

His wife agrees emphatically, "I would say so."

Alexander and Peggy are highly similar. They have identical skills and abilities. Both are analytic and good with numbers. Alexander adds, "We're both very involved with volunteerism. We believe strongly in that."

Molly and David Frost, a couple who enjoy walking, playing cards, and watching television together, acknowledge that they are essentially one person. David begins, "We think alike."

Molly maintains, "Yes, we really do."

David and Molly have participated in Marriage Encounter together, and David used that experience to demonstrate how they have similar thoughts and perceptions. "During the Marriage Encounter you do a lot of writing. And you write separately from one another. We compared notes and we wrote the same thing over and over."

Molly recalls the experience. "They give you questions, and one person goes back to the motel room, and the other stays in the large hotel room and you each answer the question. Our answers were identical most of the time. Maybe worded a little differently, but essentially the same."

When the Callahans, who enjoy verbal banter, joking, and a healthy sex life, are asked if they attempt to be separate from each other, Jim responds, "Not consciously."

Is the couple comfortable with such closeness? Jim admits, "Yeah, I think we need it."

Susie is thoughtful. "I think maybe if we had talents that went in other directions, we would have needed time alone to develop them. But we don't have any special talents."

"Do you wish you did?"

Susie responds, "I always wished that I had talent in some direction, especially in writing."

Jim interrupts, "She writes terrific poetry."

Susie throws a pillow at him, laughs, and argues, "I do not! I write lousy—I don't write at all!"

Jim smiles. "Ask Edie Busbee, she thinks it's terrific."

"I have written three poems in my entire life," Susie admits.

Jim is pleased. "But they were good; they were very good poems!"

Such exchanges mark this couple's regular interaction.

The unemotional Nortons admit they have become one by choice. Diane observes, "I could be independent, and if anything happened to him, I would be. I just don't want to be separate from him. I know how to manage everything. For instance, I take care of the checks, and now I have my Realtor's license. So actually the last six months it was my rental business that has sort of seen us through. I never wanted time for myself, to do my own thing."

Herbert's ideas are fairly similar. "I know that I'm not independent. I'm just so dependent and just used to having her around. I can do whatever I want to. If I decided I wanted to go fishing in Canada, she wouldn't be real happy about it, but she wouldn't say much. But I wouldn't do it, because I just don't want to do anything alone or with a bunch of guys. At one of the places I worked in Minneapolis, three or four nights a week, all the guys would go over to the bar and sit and drink. I couldn't see any reason why I'd work around these guys all day and then go drink with them when I could go home to my wife. So I never did. Diane's my best friend."

Diane agrees. "And he's my best friend, too."

Some couples feel they need to assert autonomy needs, but are unable to identify any areas where they thought or behaved differently. Marcia Benedik, traditional, Catholic, and midwestern, asserts, "I think we're still individuals."

Her spouse, Wayne, agrees, "Mm-hmm. We've got independent thoughts, independent ideas."

"Yeah, yeah," Marcia says.

Wayne adds, "We do not agree on everything."

I ask what topics they disagree on, but neither member of the couple can think of anything. "Politics?" I prompt.

"No." Wayne responds.

"Religion?" I try again.

"No, our religion is the same," Marcia notes.

"Can you think of any disagreements you might have?" I ask.

Wayne finally concludes, "No, I can't think of any. I don't know of any." He defends their stance, "Now this is not to say we couldn't be independent."

A few couples do establish some autonomy in their relationship. Toni Rizzo, an Italian wife of forty-eight years who enjoys both sex and dancing, begins, "We are still pretty separate people."

Joe explains, "She has more needs than I do."

Toni elaborates, "I would still travel, I would still pack up and go for two months to Japan. No adventure would be too much."

Joe, her retiring spouse, dissents, "I don't like going to airports and waiting and being shoved around. Who needs it? I'm happy doing just what I'm doing—sitting around relaxing, going shopping. I like to go out for dinners and dancing. We both like that. It doesn't take much to make me happy. I don't need more. I've had enough running."

Others recognize a need for developing separate interests. Phyllis Trent had been an elementary teacher and her husband, Ernie, had been a machinist. He was German; she was Scottish, English, and Swiss. She was the third child in a family of four while he was the middle child with nine siblings. The couple is traditional and parochial, having lived their entire life on a family homestead in a tiny township in Michigan. However, they are independent thinkers. Phyllis begins philosophically. "We start the morning together and we end the day together always. I think there is a need to get apart sometimes. I think we're like the birds. We stake out our territory. If you separate, it's awfully good when you get back together. I think you need to encourage each other to do separate things, too.''

Evelyn Ellison, a presentational septuagenarian, concurs. ''You've got to have your time alone to do your things.''

''Would twenty-four hours a day of togetherness be too much?''

She agrees at once. ''Definitely. No matter how close you are or how happy you are, you still need your time, on your end, to do your thing.''

Duncan, her reticent English spouse, adds, ''We have separate organizations and groups of people.''

• • •

The Dahlquists, another autonomous couple, had owned and operated a very successful bar and restaurant in New York state. Their three children are in their mid- to late-thirties and are all involved in some aspect of the service industry. The Dahlquists moved rarely during their marriage, have enjoyed a large home with a live-in nanny for the children, and remain active today.

Darlene explains, "I worked right with him all those years—after the kids, too. I stayed home two years after the third baby, and I almost went crazy. It wasn't me. Then we bought a house because we needed it for the three children, and we got a housekeeper and from then on it was uphill all the way. She lived in, and she was there for the kids when they were little. She was their nanny. We had two housekeepers. The first one was with us for nine years, and then her son took her to California to help him raise his little ones. Then we got another one, and she was with us seven years, and that was just enough to raise the children. And they both did a fantastic job. We were with them for breakfast and dinner every night.

"Our first housekeeper was Lydia Gripher, who's the grandmother of the man who made the 'Playground on My Mind' song popular–Clint Holmes. It was a wonderful family. She was a lovely, lovely person. She was wonderful. When she died—we don't know how old she was when she died–the children and I all went to her funeral. And they treated us like family because she lived with us for so long. She used to tease her son's children that she thought she loved our children more than her own black ones because she was with us for so long. They couldn't understand this so there was a little bit of jealousy for awhile, but when they grew up, they understood."

• • •

Some couples claim they are autonomous, but their areas of difference are primarily in the separate activities in which they engage. For instance, Courtney Salerno does craft work, interior decorating, and volunteer work, while Leo plays golf, fishes, and watches professional sports. Inga Schultz similarly does volunteer work at the area hospital, while Jergen plays tennis, does volunteer work for Hospice, and teaches classes for the Coast Guard. Jergen adds his usual barb when asked what he does each day, "I try to keep away from her."

Nancy Stouffer has a busy life of her own. She is active within her church and with civic affairs. Her walls are filled with plaques and awards underlining her important contributions. In her community she has been named "Mother of the Youth Center" and "Grandmother of the Y."

Don serves as the "neighborhood helper." Nancy explains, "Since he has so many skills, people will say, 'What do I do about this?' or 'My garage door won't open, Don,' or 'I've got a problem with my sprinkler system,' 'My disposal won't work—what plumber should I get?' We have 'Information, Please' here. The phone rings all the time. Even if they don't want him to fix it, they call and ask who they can get to do it. 'Who's the contact man for me?' It doesn't matter if it's their car, the garage door, the lawn, the pool. He's busy all the time helping someone get a contact or to help in other ways."

Don, a tall, slender, gentle person, adds, "We've inherited a batch of widows. We moved here full-time in 1970. We got acquainted with a few people, and there's been a tremendous amount of turnover and deaths. More men die than women. These widows need a lot of assistance and, boy, they don't hesitate to call."

Nancy refers to Don as the "widow's helper." During the interview, Don kept his portable phone on his lap. While the phone did not ring, his role in the neighborhood explains his need to have the phone close at hand.

Don believes the Golden Rule operates. "If she was left alone, I would appreciate the same consideration from someone else." His helping behavior may be seen as a kind of insurance for his wife after he dies.

Bradley Martin observes, "We have many things in common, but we also have many things that have nothing to do with each other. And we pursue those and try not to let it interfere. I have a number of hobbies, and she has a number of hobbies. I'm a very good cabinetmaker, for example. I'm a woodworker. I got my master's degree in electrical engineering and I'm interested in electronics. Barbara is very much interested in the stage, which I'm not interested in at all. She has always been interested in any type of dancing. We are both good ballroom dancers, but she also liked ballet and eccentric dancing. That type of thing is beyond me— I'm not an acrobat. I can't do a handstand even."

"Do you like to watch her dance?"

"Oh yeah, sure."

George and Jackie Stanowski, the youngest couple, are undoubtedly the most active. Both of them had worked. George had his own precast cement form business; Jackie worked in a hospital in charge of patient accounts. She also did bookkeeping at night. In addition, she helped her husband with his business.

While most of the couples rarely or never spent a night alone, others valued such time and actually built solitude into their routine. For example, George went from Massachusetts to Labrador fishing every year. George elaborates, "Since '55, I've been going away at least a week and sometimes two weeks. I used to spend a lot of weekends up in Vermont ice fishing. I was self-employed and my outlet was to go away from home. Otherwise the telephone would ring, and I would get all these calls. I was one of the few guys who had to get away from home. The only time I could relax was if I was away from home."

Jackie has gone on separate trips, too, but they have been relatively rare. She has gone to California with friends on vacation, and she has visited her children when a new grandchild was born. However, she prefers to travel with George. She planned on traveling to Italy with her two daughters, but when she arrived at the travel agency, she decided she didn't want to leave the country without George.

Jergen and Inga Schultz, reveal that they "live next to each other in complete harmony"; they are more independent than other couples. Their decision to engage in "parallel play" may mean they have not felt the need to become the same person. Inga is serious; Jergen plays the role of the joker.

• • •

Darlene Dahlquist has boundless energy. Less then two years ago, she agreed to become the companion for an older man, Mr. Clark. Leonard observes, "Oh, this gal, she's got energy, even Mr. Clark says so. She loves to drive, and he likes it. You know a man in his position, he wouldn't let a woman drive. Every time we go out, he says, 'Boy, you're the best, I'll let you do the driving.' "

Darlene smiles. "I have no trouble taking the keys away from him."

Leonard explains that Mr. Clark's family did not want him driving in Florida. "That was a concern of the family. Last year when he was here, he had a new Mercedes he bought and he was driving it around and I said to Darlene, 'I don't understand how this man can drive in Florida where you've got to watch yourself.' These older people, man, they're comin' out, man, they don't know what the hell they're doin'. You have to watch."

Leonard ponders a moment and then remembers that the topic is Darlene's energy level. "But she could drive day and night without stopping. I've never seen a woman with more energy and more creative energy, very artistic. Everything she does has to be just so. It drives me up a wall or I drive her up a wall because everything has to be just so or it's not done."

Darlene admits she is a perfectionist. "I'm very impatient with somebody who isn't perfect."

Leonard allows, "I'm just the opposite—see I'll take a phone call and she'll say, 'Well, who was it?' 'I don't know.' 'Why don't you write it down?' See, you can ask her what's going to happen a month from now, she'll open her date book, she'll tell you exactly what's going to happen. She's very organized."

Darlene adds, "Too much so."

• • •

The Davis couple, from central Illinois, were more autonomous when they were younger then they are today. Fred's job as a police chief and his reluctance to join the Mormon Church were partly responsible. They have found that their decreased autonomy has led to greater closeness. "Do you have a single identity rather than two separate identities?" I ask Harriet.

She responds tentatively, "I think so."

"Do you vote differently in political elections?"

"Sometimes."

Fred interjects, "We might vote in the same political party, but we will vote for different people in the same office. It's a big joke with us about whether I lost my vote or she lost hers. We both express what we're gonna do before we go. You know, when you get in the voting booth, it's private."

"Does that ever bother you that you have strong differences of opinion?"

Harriet responds quickly, "Oh no. I think it's good. I think that you need it—in your own mind—to know what you want and what's important to you."

Fred explains his political history. "I was brought up in a family that was always Democrat, and until such time as we got married, and I started to vote, and we came back to Illinois, I was a Democrat. One of my buddies in the Marine Corps ran for sheriff, and he was running on the Republican ticket, and so I voted for him in the primary, and my father and mother would not even talk to me 'cause I'd registered as a Republican. But over the years, I've become a Republican because the people that I believe in and feel that can do the best job in office are Republicans."

He continues, "I know Harriet votes differently than I do sometimes. I tell her how I feel; she tells me how she feels. Like I say, when we get in that booth, that's our own business."

"Are there other areas of disagreement?"

Fred begins another story. "She's been a Mormon all her life and I was not. I just joined ten years ago. It was the best thing that ever happened to me because up till that time I drank coffee, drank beer, smoked, and the Mormon Church doesn't believe in any of that. I realized at that time that this was the best thing, if I could do it. I didn't even tell her that I was going to join till the day before.

"When the kids were little, she took them to church. I prepared the meals on Sunday when they were gone. I went to church after the kids left home. I went with her for six or seven years before I joined. I didn't tell her until the day before when I was gonna be baptized, Saturday afternoon. It was a surprise for her. I knew it'd make her happy, I really did. But I had decided that smoking wasn't good for me, that coffee wasn't good for me, and drinking booze didn't do it anymore for me, either. There was no way I could join a church till I made up my mind that I was not a hypocrite. When I made up my mind finally to do it, I knew she would be tickled to death, and she's been tickled ever since.

"I could not wait then, from the time I joined the church— you have to wait a year—before we could go to the temple to be remarried for time and eternity. I couldn't wait then till that year was over till we could go to the temple. Since then, we try to go at least once, and sometimes twice, a year to the closest temple. It made us a lot closer. Being remarried in the church made more of a bond than before."

• • •

The Dahlquists are clearly in a new phase of their marriage. While they had worked side by side for most of their marriage, Darlene now has a job that takes her away from Leonard. Leonard agreed to her new career, even though it meant that the couple had to live apart for a number of months during the past winter. Darlene accompanied Mr. Clark to Florida while Leonard stayed in New York. This separation was devastating for Leonard.

Leonard recounts the story of their recent change. "She left with Mr. Clark [the older man for whom she serves as a companion in Florida] in October and, of course, I'm staying at the club [in New York] until after the Christmas holidays. Just three months, I'm away from her, right? And I'm going crazy. I can't stand it. The last thing that happened to me was hives. I had to go to the dermatologist. My whole body was going. I said, 'What the hell is wrong with me?' I went to my regular doctor and he said, 'I don't know, Len, maybe it's because Darlene is away.'"

Leonard addresses his spouse. "You know it felt like you were gone about two years or something. It affected me so much."

He returns to his story. "Finally, my internist said to me, 'You've got to go to a dermatologist because I can't handle what you've got.' So I went to the dermatologist and he took care of it for me. I told him the same thing. It's probably nerves or something that's bothering me because my wife is away. I just couldn't handle it for awhile. Once I got it straightened out, then I came to Florida, then I was great. It's wonderful."

Did Darlene experience any separation anxiety?

She looks surprised. "No, I'm too independent. I relaxed. I enjoyed my aloneness. The one thing I miss now is that I don't have any alone time. In our big house, you could go to the basement, you could go on the terrace, you could go into the bedroom and read and be alone.

"Then we got an apartment, and we were just like lovebirds, holding hands and experiencing a whole new life because we moved into a new community. That lasted three months. We were told Mom had to come and live with us, and there was no place to go. We were three adults in an apartment. We had begged her for years to come and live with us in the big house, when we had all this room and everybody was gone. It didn't happen *then. It happened when we moved to a small apartment, and then there was all this togetherness. I didn't have a place to hide.*

"So my three months without him, and I think he knows this, if I haven't told him, I enjoyed every minute of it. Especially since I was only working nine to five. I would come home, sit on the terrace, have a cocktail, watch the water, and just think, 'Isn't this marvelous?' No mother, no husband, no children, no nothing. Just me. So I thoroughly recouped.

"By the time our daughter came with him in January, she said, 'Mother, you're so relaxed.' I said, 'I have had time to regroup. I had a chance to relax. I had a time to read when I wanted to read, to do needlework, to do this, to do that.' She said, 'Boy, what a change.' So this was good. I really don't miss him. I'm sure I would have—eventually.

"He was so upset when he was first operated on [they have both had bypass surgery]—Leonard had never been sick in his life. He was sure that any minute he was going to drop dead, after the surgery. He was quite morbid. He was very, very depressed for a long time. He couldn't cope with it. I'd say, 'Let's not go on this vacation this year. Let's collect our thoughts. We have this nice new apartment. Let's save some money. Just enjoy.' 'Oh no, I may be dead tomorrow.' That would drag me down and I'd say, 'All right, I'll go.'

"But when I was away this time, he would be so upset. One day he called and he had this horrendous cold and he said, 'I can't shake this cold.' Then the hives. I said, 'Now listen, I may die before you. We both had bypass surgery. I'm the one who's smoking like a fiend. I can't give it up. I'll probably die first, so pretend this is a dress rehearsal for when I'm dead. You have to learn to live by yourself.'

"Whether that meant anything to him or not, I don't know, but I told the children that, because he would bother the children, of course. I preached to him all of the time. 'Don't do what my mother did to me, and make a slave of the children. Learn to live by yourself. Pay your own bills, do your own laundry.' I had done everything for him. I don't know if that helped or not."

Apparently, it did not. Leonard reveals, "Nothing helped. The closer I got to the time of coming, I was more settled."

Darlene adds, "The children tried to get him to go to the various parties and functions and he'd say, 'I have no time.' But then he'd be sitting home, calling me. I'd say, 'Write yourself notes, what you want to ask me, and call me on Saturday or Sunday when the rates are down.' But every morning, he'd call me. The telephone bill was horrendous! But he couldn't help himself. He had to call me. I'd be aggravated, but I couldn't help but admit that I was glad to think that he would call."

"It sounds like Leonard sees the two of you as one person and that half of this person was missing. However, Darlene you seem highly autonomous," I conclude.

Darlene takes the observation in stride. "Don't you think that's typical of women?"

• • •

Only four of the couples interviewed showed that autonomy was critical in their happy marriages. These four include the Dahlquists, featured in this chapter, the Gronbecks, the Neilsens, and the Silvers. In all cases, the autonomy was exhibited primarily by the women. Three of the women worked, albeit later in their marriages, while the fourth was an assertive, argumentative person who would not be dominated by another.

Patricia Gronbeck, from Wisconsin, begins, "I think there's a limit to togetherness at some point."

Although Carl, her spouse, is essentially retired, when he returns to Beaver Dam, Wisconsin, during the summer and autumn months, he resumes a normal workday schedule. The other six months a year, which they spend in Florida, they are generally together. Carl spends a great deal of time reading. He subscribes to twenty-one magazines each month, and he also goes to the public library and reads both books and newspapers.

Patricia Gronbeck is a woman ahead of her time. She states frankly, "I'm really a believer of a working woman. I know it's good for them to stay home with their kids and so forth, and being a kindergarten teacher, I can attest that it is. But a woman has to have an identity of her own."

Carl adds, "I felt that the longer I was in my job, I was growing considerably. It was nice to see Patricia go back to school and see her develop. In all due modesty, Patricia was one of the best teachers I have ever seen. I know she'll blush a little bit. Basically, she was just ahead of her time."

Patricia continues, "In retrospect, looking back, I think it would have been good if I could have started working a little earlier. It wasn't possible with Carl gone so much and with the children being so young."

Although Patricia is a strong and independent-minded woman, Carl is not simply ditto marks for her. The two disagree on political and civic issues. Carl has always written letters to the editor and taken strong stands on civic, state, and national issues. Carl admits that he no longer gets involved in every issue. When asked if it was because he had mellowed with age, Patricia announces, "No, it was because I put the finger on it. If I can. It's usually in the paper before I can see it."

The two laugh and Carl adds, "I never show it to her. I draft all of these letters, and I reread them, and sometimes I hold them for a little while, but I don't tell her about them. She doesn't know I wrote the letter until she reads it in the newspaper."

This couple clearly believes in the importance of autonomy for both men and women.

The Silvers from New York City are autonomous, but they defy categorization. They represented one of the couples with strong autonomy needs, but they also illustrated in their behavior and their words their inclination toward merging. (We will discuss evidence of their autonomy here and feature them in the next chapter on verbal intimacy, as well.)

One way that married couples maintain their autonomy is through separate friendships. Although both Ari and Ruth Ann Silver had earlier stated that they have no separate friends, later in the interview they admit that they each have one unique friend, not shared by the other.

Ruth Ann's friend is someone she worked with over thirty years before. Ari's friend is someone who was with him in therapy. However, neither Ruth Ann nor Ari particularly care for the other's exclusive friend. Ruth Ann notes, "We treat each other with a certain amount of respect. I don't interfere with his relationship with Mike. I don't understand it, and Mike would not be my favorite person."

Ari adds, "She doesn't like his wife, either."

Ruth Ann is vehement, "I can't stand his wife." She goes on, "But we each treat the relationship between the men with a certain amount of respect. They have a good thing going. So we don't interfere."

Ari interjects, "And I don't interfere with her relationship."

"And he doesn't interfere with my relationship," Ruth Ann adds.

Ari continues, "Whose husband is a tremendous bore."

"Yes, he is that," Ruth Ann says. "But she and I are very close."

I ask the couple directly about their inclination to be autonomous. Ari thinks about the question and responds quickly, "I don't think Ruth Ann is a separate person."

Ruth Ann is not pleased. "What?"

Ari explains, "I'm sorry. I'm sorry, but you don't go to beauty parlors, you don't sit with women, you're not interested in mah jongg, you're not interested in sewing clubs, you have no interest in separateness at all. If I'm not included, you don't even want to do it."

Ruth Ann adds, "I'm not interested in women's games. I'm not terribly fond of women. Most of our friends have been men."

Ari stipulates, "Single men, divorced men, gay men."

Ruth Ann notes, "I get along very well with men, on a non-sexual basis."

"There are a lot of women we know who are single, divorced and gay," Ari suggests.

Ruth Ann quickly responds, "But I don't have that kind of relationship with them. He gets along much better with men than I do with women."

Ruth Ann is happy to admit that she is "a man's woman" rather than "a woman's woman" and took more of her identity from traditional masculine activities and characteristics. She does not share her husband's perception that she is not autonomous. She argues with him, "I have more of an identity then you do."

Ari declines to accept her remark. "I don't agree at all." He turns to me and offers, "She won't get involved in anything that doesn't involve me whereas I will get involved with things that don't involve her."

I ask Ari for some examples, and he is quick to offer illustrations. "I used to go fishing, I used to go swimming, without her. She would always say, 'Where were you? It took you so long.' "

Ruth Ann suggests her question should not have been viewed as disapproval. "He has always misunderstood that facet of our relationship. I am a very literal person. If you say you are going to be here at one-thirty, I expect you to be here at one-thirty. He goes out fishing with his friends, I say 'What time do you expect to be back?' He says, 'Between four and four-thirty.' But then he comes back at six o'clock. I am more than annoyed. I say, 'What took you so long?' He misunderstands. He was not punctual. But I was perfectly agreeable to his going."

"I had a boat with a friend," Ari says. "We shared a boat. She doesn't like boats so we [he and his friend] used to go boating together. She always resented the fact that I was away on the boat."

Ruth Ann shoots back, "You know that isn't true."

Ari does not acquiesce. "Oh yes. She was so happy when I sold that boat."

Ruth Ann finally admits, "Well we nearly died in that boat."

He alleges, "That's something else."

Ruth Ann repeats, "That's something else" and attempts to establish her identity. "I don't have any trouble preserving my 'me.' I know who I am. I don't know if Ari understands the question. I think he is deliberately misunderstanding. I am a very strong-willed 'me.' We have no problem maintaining our separate identities."

Ari asserts, "I have a very different inner life-style."

Ruth Ann immediately agrees. "He does. He's very different from me."

"We see two different worlds."

Ruth Ann shifts gears. "We are very different, but we complement each other." Ari provides an example of how each perceives the world. "When we're watching a movie, I say this is happening, and this is the thought and the theme of the movie. She will not only disagree with me, but she'll tell me I'm dead wrong. Now how can I be dead wrong, when that's how I feel about it? I respect her interpretation. She may be right, and I may be wrong."

"On the other hand," Ruth Ann admits, "I respect him, too."

Ari will have none of it. "You don't respect my interpretation."

"That isn't true."

I became confused. "Do people say you have a good marriage?" I inquire.

At once Ari relates, "People are very envious of our relationship. They think we're wonderful."

Ruth Ann adds, "They also think we look alike."

Ari assents, "We do. We even look like our dog. We're short, fat people."

"You're resilient," I conclude as I pack up my materials to leave.

• • •

Leonard Dahlquist is intuitive and relaxed. As he moves around his home, he whistles happily to himself. Leonard says, "Well, I'm easy going, I flow with the tide. Nothing excites me, really excites me. I go along with anything that she wants or does. I think that's why we get along so well. I don't think it would work out so well if she was with someone who was like she is. That would be a mess."

Darlene disagrees. "I think it would be all right for both of us. Under the circumstances, it's just that you have an entirely different life. Your life-style would be one way and my life-style would be completely different. You seem to temper me and I seem to temper you. We complement each other. That's my theory. We each have something that the other one doesn't have, so it works."

• • •

Researchers, and their models of effective family functioning, recommend some autonomy in a satisfying relationship. Couples married forty-forever years do not appear to have the same need for autonomy suggested by the theories and the research done on younger couples. Two explanations are in order. First, these couples may have had greater autonomy needs when they were younger then they do in their sixties, seventies, and eighties. Too, they may have merged because of their long relational history.

Another explanation deals with sex-role crossover, which begins for most people in their forties and continues throughout the rest of the life span. Both women and men experience this crossover, which encourages women to become more masculine and men to become increasingly feminine. The stereotyped and negative picture is the older woman aggressively fighting her way through shopping mall crowds while her husband shuffles behind holding her handbag. The positive view includes grandfathers who are highly nurturing to their grandchildren, even though they were not so caring in their attention to their own children. Also encouraging are the increasing numbers of older women who find successful careers after the age of forty.

The sex-role crossover may account for the finding that the only couples who demonstrated any marked need for individuality occurred because the women needed more independence and freedom. The men were not demanding, nor even necessarily encouraging, the separateness between themselves and their wives. On the other hand, the men were flexible. Some of the husbands engaged in "relational flexing" just as their wives did. The sex-role crossover may also encourage greater closeness, as both men and women have the opportunity of seeing the world from the other person's perspective. Men may understand better the frustration of housecleaning when the house simply gets dirty again, while women might empathize with the difficulty of the competitive, traditionally male work world.

Happily married couples may require varied levels of autonomy. Older couples who have long and happy marriages and who married in the 1930s and 1940s appear to generally have a decreased need for autonomy than do the general population of married couples. The long and rich relational history of the long-term happily marrieds may partially account for their decreased needs in this area.

Younger happily married couples might vary on this marital need. The need for increased autonomy may be a communicative behavior reserved for younger couples, for unhappy couples, or for both. At the same time, even a few of these couples illustrated that one individual's need for autonomy could be incorporated into a long and happy marriage.

Couples need both to remain two separate people as well as become one identity. These are not competing ideas, although there is sometimes tension between the pull to become one and the desire to remain as two. In this chapter, we considered how satisfied couples maintained their autonomy. In the next chapter, we detail how they become one through verbal intimacy and shared secrets.

Chapter 7

Becoming One: "A Two-Headed Animal"

In order to see I have to be willing to be seen.

—Hugh Prather

The serene symphony sound that you hear before the door is opened contrasts with the pugnacious pug that barks and jumps after you are greeted at the door by Aaron "Ari" Silver. Ari ushers you into a lanai and Ruth Ann shuts off the stereo.

Although Ruth Ann hangs back at the doorway, she does not hang back in her conversation with you. She is just over 5' tall, and probably weighs about 130 pounds, which renders her pudgy. She has short, somewhat curly blonde hair that frames her face. Is it real or is it a wig? The hairstyle is later explained when Ruth Ann discloses that she has had a facelift. Clearly, the style is adopted to hide scars along the hairline. Ruth Ann's eyes are large and brown. She does not wear glasses. Her chin is slight, which adds to her round-faced, round-bellied look. Her skin—not surprisingly after her disclosure—is far smoother than the skin of most septuagenarians.

Ari is 5'4" at the outside. Both his height and his rheumy blue eyes make him appear vulnerable; however, his comments during the interview show him to be a combative communicator. Ari has a receding chin and a great deal of extra skin at the neck. He wears glasses, is somewhat wrinkled, and has dark hair. He looks a great deal like Maude's husband on the situation comedy of the 1970s of the same name.

The couple both do resemble each other and their pug dog, who sleeps on Ruth Ann's lap. They are short and stubby, but pugnacious and unrestrained. They are quick to bark, but not to bite. They have been married forty-nine years and are seventy-two years old.

Ruth Ann Silver explains their long marriage. "We have become a two-headed animal. When he has a pain, I hurt. When he wakes up in the night, I wake up, too. It's a very strange relationship." She laughs. "I think we need a doctor."

• • •

Verbal intimacy involves being so well acquainted with each other that words are often unnecessary. It also includes openness and honesty. A decade ago, marital counselors preached total openness and honesty; today, they are not so sure. What do couples in long-term marriages advise? Do they share everything? When are they open and honest and when are they closed and less than honest? What topics are taboo? We will learn the answers from successfully married couples in this chapter on verbal intimacy.

Intimacy refers to our close relationships, associations, affiliations, or acquaintances with other people. Intimacy suggests two people share personal, private, informal, or secret information. Intimacy is important in satisfying marriages. Sven Wahlroos concurs. "An emotionally healthy person is able to give of himself fully in deep and lasting emotional relationships." He contrasts the emotionally healthy person with the narcissist:

> The opposite of an emotionally healthy person. . .would be the narcissist, the one who sees other people only in terms of whether they could be of use to him or not. To a narcissist, other people possess no intrinsic worth, they exist only as pleasure-providers or obstacle-placers. . . .a narcissist creates his own tragedy: he can never experience a satisfying emotional relationship with another human being, unless he is willing to see his narcissism as the problem it is.

Pepper Schwartz and Donna Jackson received over 15,000 responses from married women who read *New Woman*. Their respondents, primarily between twenty-five and forty-four years of age, are younger than the people interviewed for this book. Too, their marriages are far shorter, since the median length of these marriages is six years. From these women, the researchers construct a model of three features that describe the model marriage.

In the February, 1989, issue of *New Woman*, the researchers report that one of the factors is spending quality time together. They observe, "A relationship needs time—time for mutual interests to develop, time to discuss issues both partners care about, time to notice and work on problems that arise. The less time a couple spends together, the less happy the partners are." Similarly, the Consumers Union determines, that "Open communications between wife and husband . . .provide an almost iron-clad guarantee of a happy marriage."

People surveyed by *USA Today* agree with the experts. Couples identified those factors most important to maintaining a good relationship with their mate. Among the most important factors were honesty (identified by 96 percent of those polled), discussing feelings (identified by 95 percent), sharing financial goals (65 percent), sharing religious values (52 percent), and sharing career goals (42 percent). These behaviors are related to talking to family members and to providing self-disclosure, which allow intimacy. These behaviors encourage marital satisfaction.

Communication, in and of itself, is related to satisfying relationships. Couples who talk to each other tend to be more satisfied than couples who do not talk to each other. Open communication affects the quality of marriage. Overall marital happiness is highly related to the couple's ability to discuss problems effectively and to share their feelings.

However, marital partners may talk to each other far less than they realize. One researcher found that of the 10,080 minutes in each week, the average couple spends about seventeen minutes talking to each other. The contemporary, younger couple are often rarely at home at the same time. They also often spend a great deal of their busy day interacting with others, so additional time spent in communication is not necessarily seen as inviting.

In addition, husbands and wives may overestimate how much they disclose to each other. The knowledge one partner accumulates about the other in the relationship may be based more on the other's behavior and on their relational history than on his or her self-disclosure. This appears to be particularly true in marriages that span forty years or more.

Nonetheless, satisfied couples tend to interact more than dissatisfied couples. The content of their talk is different, too. Happier couples talk about important personal matters, while unhappy couples talk about mundane issues or they gossip about others.

• • •

How did the Silvers, who resemble their pug dog, meet? Ruth Ann was working for Ari. He remembers, "We met in an office where I was an executive and she was in the typing pool. We met, and we married three months after we met."

When I asked them if they had been engaged, Ruth Ann quickly responds, "I was." She went on to explain that she had been engaged to someone else when she met Ari.

"Yeah, but he didn't want to set a date," Ari notes.

"That isn't what happened at all," Ruth Ann interrupts. "Ari always has his own version of what happened."

Ari continues, undaunted, "Well he didn't set the date, and I was being drafted."

Ruth Ann tries again. "Darling, that isn't what happened at all. The war was on and everybody was thinking about the draft, and he was, too. I had been seeing this man for a couple of years, and it was expected that we would marry. And we assumed we would, too. Then along came this Lothario, and he literally swept me off my feet. In the middle of my relationship with this other guy, one day I decided to accept his proposal and marry him. That's how it happened."

What attracted Ruth Ann and Ari to each other? He quips, "My money." However, Ruth Ann remembers clearly that they each had thirty-five dollars in the bank at the time, and Ari agrees. Ari tries a second answer. "I think it was sex more than anything."

Ruth Ann quickly affirms, "I think it was sex. It wasn't personality—in three months you can scarcely know each other. We were kids, we were very inexperienced. We had absolutely no idea what we were doing, but there was such a strong attraction between us that we couldn't resist each other. So we got married." Were they engaged to each other? Ruth Ann jokes, "For a couple of weeks."

• • •

Self-disclosure occurs when we offer verbal revelations about ourselves to others. It is voluntary, intentional, and accurate information that we provide another person that he or she is unlikely to know or to find out from another source. Self-disclosure requires some risk. It renders one person vulnerable to another.

Do couples in long and satisfying marriages tell their partners everything? Many claim they do. The supportive Laura Clausen answers automatically, "I tell him everything. I'm very open." Her response is typical of many satisfied spouses.

One reason couples married forty years or more are so disclosive is that they spend most of their time together. Largely because of retirement, most of the couples are free to spend a great deal of time together. Some of the happily married older couples state that they spent almost no time away from each other. Two-thirds of the couples spend twenty or more hours together each day.

The amount of time they spend together allows for increased disclosure and it increases their marital satisfaction as well. Recent studies generally show that couples who spend more time together, talk to each other more often, and focus more frequently on important private topics are more satisfied than those who spend little time together, do not talk to each other, and talk only about superficial topics. Contrary to the maxim, talk is not cheap.

Although openness is generally desirable between partners seeking happiness, some caution is in order. Douglas L. Kelley, from Seattle Pacific University, reminds us that "Oneness, or bondedness, does not imply loss of one's self." He adds, "The family should function to help develop individuals' identities." A similar idea is provided by the textbook authors Kathy Galvin and Bernie Brommel, who hold that the family functions to develop at least two themes: (1) how to interact with others, and (2) how to develop personally. Leslie Baxter, from the University of California at Davis, and Kathryn Dindia, at the University of Wisconsin–Milwaukee, observe, "Relationship parties face ongoing . . . tension between the need for open disclosure coupled with the need for information discretion." Couples want to be open with each other, but they also recognize that some information may not be appropriate to share.

Some satisfied couples share everything and feel little need for information discretion. However, other couples experience such a need. Many identify topics, emotions, or other items that they simply do not discuss with their partner. Many men do, or did, not bring home problems from work or share typically male experiences, such as their war or hunting experiences. For instance, Leo Salerno did not share his work problems with Courtney when he was working because he didn't want to burden her with what he perceived to be his problems. Similarly, he did not share his war experiences.

Don Stouffer, formerly in the meat business, did not share all of his work problems or gossip with Nancy. She adds that he had been an avid hunter when he was younger, and the activities that surrounded hunting and their hunting cabin were kept among the men who hunted with him. Jane notes, "That was a life unto his own. It was his own thing."

The dentist Walter Clausen felt that he could not ethically tell Laura some things that occurred at work. "As a professional, you just don't carry a lot of those things. Let me give you an example of a tough situation in a town where I practiced, where my patients are not only my patients but our social friends or our good friends. The young daughter comes into the office and tells the hygienist, 'I don't want X rays, I'm pregnant.' 'Does your mother know about it?' 'No, my mother and father don't know.'

"I was out of the office that day and I call the young woman back to the office and talk to her personally. I said to her, 'The first people you have to tell are your parents. Will you promise me when you leave this office you will tell your parents, who are our friends, too? I will go with you.' She did not go tell her parents, but I could not tell them, either."

Laura interjects, bringing him back to the topic, "But he didn't tell me, either. Which I respect. The first thing you learn in nursing is you don't repeat things."

Walter agrees, "You don't tell your spouse everything."

Laura adds, "But being a professional, I really respect that. I admire that in somebody."

Walter smiles, "Even though you'd say, 'Why didn't you tell me?'"

Laura laughs. "I asked, 'Am I the last one to know?'"

Similarly, some women prefer to talk with other women about uniquely feminine experiences. At first, Fred and Harriet Davis, from Urbana, Illinois, cannot identify any topics they did not share. Harriet begins, "I don't know. There isn't anything that we wouldn't discuss with one another if we felt the need. But it's always nice to have somebody else to talk to, too. We've always been fortunate to have very close friends."

Fred provides an illustration. "I think a good example is that she had a hysterectomy the sixth of January, a complete one, and she was able to talk to a lot of women, in part, because they'd had it. And to me, it wasn't a common experience because I didn't know what they were talking about other than what the doctor told me. It was nice that she could express her feelings and other people could express their feelings to her. They told her she was gonna have a lot of pain, but she would get over it and it would be well worth it in the long run."

What are other reasons for holding back? Some couples show sensitivity for their partner. They recognize that some of their experiences might be viewed as less than interesting. Family therapist Julia Neilsen comments, "It's not that there's anything that I'm afraid to talk about, but I don't need to share everything. I don't have to provide every detail."

Her husband, Ben, who had graduated from West Point, agrees. "Some of those things are part of your individual life, which you don't need to share. It partly matters whether she's interested or not. I can see a glazed look in her eyes when I go on about some things and I know I've gone too far. Why do I unload on her? That's not fair to her if she's not interested. She's been a good soldier and pretty soon she's going to tell me something and she does: 'Hey, hold it!' "

Many of the couples identify gossip or hurtful remarks about others as a topic that is verboten. Leo Salerno does not like catty remarks; he will not repeat such comments to Courtney either. He notes, "Sometimes you'll be out and you'll hear bickering among your mutual friends. I let it lay. I don't like to hear it and I won't repeat it."

Laura Clausen recalls, "I used to say to him, 'But Walt, you must have known about this.' Speaking of gossip, I don't like gossip, either. I have friends who thrive on it. I would be more likely to tell him something I heard than he would to tell me."

Some of the couples protect their partner. George Stanowski, who had been self-employed in the cement business, did not like to hear negative information. Jackie remembers, "I kept telling him how lucky he was [that their children were so good during the teenage years] and he said, 'I don't want to hear it, I expect them to be good.' "

Jackie said that George did not want to talk when they came home from work, either. George defends himself, "Every time she came home, she had bad news. I said, 'I don't want to listen. Tell me somebody made a million dollars and is happy about it. I'm not listening to somebody dying.' I want to hear something good about somebody; I don't want to hear about the bad."

Jackie laughs and explains that bad news is more prevalent than good news in the admissions section of the hospital at which she worked. But she adds, seriously, "He didn't know about the real world, about people with real problems. I tried to explain to him, 'You don't know how lucky we are.' He thinks the whole world is rosy." As we have seen from the comments of other couples, one of the secrets of success in long-term marriages is viewing the world through rose-colored glasses.

Walter Clausen, too, notes that he protected Laura. "I'm more likely not to say something if it's going to be upsetting."

Diana Norton, mother of six from Minneapolis, Minnesota, protected Herbert, and she encouraged their children to respect him, too. She explains, "I always taught the kids, 'Don't talk to your father until he's eaten supper.'" She smiles, "And some of them remembered it."

Herb adds, "Or if you talked to me, you just couldn't bring bad news."

Diane summarizes, "Don't bring bad news. Don't mention anything until after he's eaten. Six kids chargin' at the door. I don't think I learned that from anybody. It just seems like a mean thing to do when he's tired at the end of the day."

Some couples cannot, or do not, share particular feelings. Cookie Simonian, who is warm and effusive, offers a surprising revelation. She begins, "I never show my feelings. In fact when we lost my daughter, he almost had a nervous breakdown. Our [other] daughter says, 'I know that someday the two of you have to go, but I pray Dad goes before you because Dad would never be able to take it. I know he would never be able to cope.'"

Sam asserts, "We are going together."

For the Scandinavian Nortons, negative expressions are forbidden. I ask, "If you were feeling badly, would you share that with each other?"

Diane looks truly puzzled. "I guess I don't ever recall feeling that way."

Herb shares, "We've gone through some periods in the past few months of indecision because the place here is going through receivership, and it would be very easy to get down in the dumps about it, because there's no income and we don't know what's gonna happen, or anything. We talk about it and if anything, she picks me up, if it looks like I'm feeling down. But we have both made a habit not to feel grumpy. A lot of people use moodiness as a defense mechanism, where actually it's an aggressive mechanism. They feel if they get in a bad mood, everybody's gonna get out of their way." The Nortons, like other couples, prefer a positive outlook. They may not have been given a rose garden, but their view of life is rosy.

On the other hand, the Neilsens recognize that not sharing certain emotions was damaging to them in the early days of their marriage. Julia recalls, "Oh, yeah, I never talked about my anger. The first time, after this change [she met Virginia Satir and became a family therapist, which changed their marriage dramatically] had come about, I yelled at him to 'shut up.' Then I left the room. I came back ten minutes later, and he was laughing."

Ben has his own memories. "For the first twenty years, I never shared my anger. I never talked to her about my anger about being on a leash, feeling controlled by her."

Both members of this couple had felt controlled by the other.

Julia reflects on this. "I think it was a power struggle."

Ben explains, "Like early in the marriage, one way that I unconsciously—I don't see how you could do it consciously—is that I would get out of an engagement that was already agreed on by having a severe headache or severe stomachache or something. It was genuine and real, and I don't know how you can induce that. It would happen a lot of time on the weekend or on the weeknights after the work was done or after the essential work was done. 'You want me to drive to New York and go somewhere or another?' I'd be quiet."

Julia recalls her feelings. "I'd be mad as hell because we'd already agreed, and how could I tell the others?"

Although early studies recommended total openness and honesty, more recent writing is cautious in encouraging total self-disclosure. Two researchers, Gilbert and Horenstein, write, ". . . the communication of intimacies is a behavior which has positive effects only in limited, appropriate circumstances. . . . 'the transparent self' is not, perhaps, the ideal model for all people."

Simply saying more will not result in increased marital satisfaction. Couples are better advised to be selective. Research shows that couples who disclose information that deals with the two of them are more satisfied than couples who disclose information that is more individually based.

What affects the relationship between self-disclosure and satisfaction? First, expectation levels affect the appropriateness of disclosure. If you are not accustomed to sharing your thoughts, ideas, and feelings with your spouse, he or she may be upset rather than pleased if you suddenly "tell all." The history of the relationship must be kept in mind.

Negative information may be best left undisclosed, too. For instance, two researchers found unhappy couples disclose more unpleasant feelings than satisfied couples. They conclude that

> talking about one's feelings does not necessarily refer to spilling out everything. For the average couple, *selective disclosure* of feelings seems more beneficial to marital harmony than indiscriminate catharsis.

Happier spouses report less disclosure of negative feelings toward their mates, in particular, and less negative disclosure, in general. Recently, an investigator recommended, "If the disclosure is negative, hostile, is viewed as nagging, and/or excessive concern about the self, less may be better." Apparently, what they don't know, can help 'em.

Unsolicited criticism should be avoided. Farrell writes, "Unsolicited criticism in the name of honesty can be like a punch in the stomach for which we are unprepared." He adds, "The great magician Houdini died of such a punch from a fan who didn't allow Houdini time to prepare himself."

Are all negative feelings out of bounds for the couple who desires satisfaction? Certainly not. One study, for instance, determined that couples can discuss some unpleasant topics and receive positive responses. When individuals disclose vulnerabilities or hostilities about people other than the listener, the spouse is likely to respond positively.

Total disclosure is not necessary for a satisfying relationship. We might guess that total honesty, however, is a necessary condition. Many couples who had experienced long and happy marriages would not agree with us. A number of the marriages are begun on a "white lie" or an exaggeration. Carl and Patricia Gronbeck, the insurance person and the schoolteacher, met at a dance on Valentine's Day at the University of Wisconsin, which they both attended. Carl was a first year student, but because he had been in the service, he was older than most of the other students in that class. Patricia was a sophomore, and he told her when they met that he was a senior majoring in engineering. Patricia worked for the residence hall and had access to all students' records. Carl recalls, "I got caught the first night in a lie, so I have never lied since."

Patricia asks, "Is his nose twitching?"

Similarly, Jane and Kenneth Harris, the rugged individualists, began their relationship with dishonesty. She believed Ken's navy records, which listed him as four years older then he actually was. Ken did not bother to correct this misunderstanding. Other satisfied couples, too, did not know "the truth, the whole truth" about their spouse before they wed.

In some instances, couples do not share information in order to have some fun with each other. Herbert Norton, father of six, recounts such an incident. "Just last week, our daughter called to say she got an engagement ring. This is the one who's never been married."

Herbert smiles, "And I thought it would be kind of funny if our cousin who lives on Marco—she spills everything—if she knew and Diane did not. So she called just afterward, and I told her about it. She said, 'Well, we'll have something to celebrate.' But I didn't bother to tell Diane—on purpose. That night we were playing cards with our cousin and her husband. We were sitting playing cards, and the daughter called back and Diane answered the phone and the daughter said, 'Say, I think Dad probably didn't tell you,' cause she could just read me. She knew what was going on. So, she told Diane then."

Diane shakes her head. "She said, 'I don't want you to hear this from somebody else,' so she told me, and I had to sit here, and Herb was sitting here, and I had to pretend it was some other call, because I didn't want him to know that I knew. We were just playing a joke."

Herbert acknowledges, "We'll play a little game like that once in awhile, but other than that, I don't know of anything we don't talk about."

Many older couples cannot play such jokes on each other because of their capacity to read each other's thoughts and to predict what and how the other person feels. Most successful couples comment on their ability to "mind read." Without saying a word, one partner knows what the other is thinking. In other cases, one partner would say a word or two which would prompt the second to respond in predictable ways. Ruth Ann Silver's disclosure at the beginning of this chapter serves as an example.

Leo Salerno, the man who waxes poetic, notes, "We are so close, sometimes it frightens me. I'll be sitting here and thinking of something and she will come out and say it. ESP is one thing, but this just boggles your mind. It doesn't just happen infrequently. It can happen two or three times a week. I just thought about it, and she comes out and says it!"

His wife, Courtney, adds another example. "How about buying cards? We will buy the same cards for each other, not knowing. Anniversary cards, it's unbelievable. So that's how much we think alike. It's weird sometimes."

Hugh O'Brien, the Irishman from Massachusetts, discusses the ability he and Mary Carol have of understanding each other. "By now we can almost read each other's mind. It doesn't bother me, but it amazes me sometimes." Hugh humorously notes it might be a sign of a good marriage, but it almost might occur because older couples keep repeating themselves all the time and they can predict because they remember what the other person said the last time.

Bill Cosby suggests that same phenomenon:

"Where are you going? I say to her as she gets up from a dinner table and starts to leave people I'm entertaining.

"To anyplace," she softly says, "where I won't have to hear this story for the ninety-seventh time."

This moment reveals the ultimate challenge for a woman in marriage: to accept it for the rerun it is but keep herself from canceling the show.

Jergen and Inga Schultz, born in Germany, are two halves of a whole. Inga states, "We never speak in full sentences. He says one word and I know how to answer. He says, 'Where,' and I know what he's talking about. For instance on Thursday, he said, 'Where,' and I said, 'You decided last week.' It's like a code."

The Schultzes are a very close couple. Indeed, Inga observes that one of the problems they will have when one of them dies is that they are so interdependent. She asserts, "We don't need other people. We are perfectly happy. We could be home all week long or do things alone without having people in the house or without going out. It wouldn't bother us. We are very selective with our friends. We basically do not need people. This is something that worries us for either one—what will happen when one of us dies?"

Nancy and Don Stouffer have "sympathy pains" when the other partner is ill. Nancy laughs. "He has sympathy illness. He always is as sick as I am. He has such a sympatico with me that he knows when I am not well. He's very, very attuned." Although Nancy looks fit, she has had many surgeries. She developed cancer first when she was thirty-five years of age and has continued to develop a variety of cancers. She is currently being examined for potential bone cancer.

Many satisfied couples engage in mind reading. At the same time, being able to read the other person's mind is not an expectation of people in happy relationships. Current studies show that requiring your partner to be able to know your thoughts without expressing them is harmful to the relationship. Mind reading may be a gift of a long and satisfying marriage; it cannot be viewed as an automatic benefit provided with the job.

• • •

The Jewish Silvers grew up in New York City and remained there until retirement. They are each only children; he the son of immigrants and she the daughter of people who had been in the country for some time. Ruth Ann completed high school, and Ari attended college for two years. When he retired, he was a successful manager with a large publishing house in New York. When they met, she was a secretary.

Although raised within the Jewish faith, they never attended synagogue and Ari claims he is an agnostic or an atheist "depending on how my health is." Ruth Ann professes a belief in God. While the couple has no children of their own, they adopted a ten-year-old boy whose mother and whose father had died. They treat this grown child as their own.

The Silvers are the only couple interviewed who claim they spend twenty-four hours a day together. They shop, swim in the nude in their own pool, sunbathe, and go on walks every day. They clean the house together, prepare and eat meals together, and have drinks and coffee. They enjoy travel, con-

certs, playing cards, and entertaining. They believe their marriage has lasted so long because of common interests. Ruth Ann and Ari Silver have few separate interests or friends. She explains, "We spend all our time together. I don't know if that's true of all married people. Whatever we do, we do together."

Although retirement allows more time together, Ari and Ruth Ann were together a great deal before retirement, too. She recalls, "Even early on in our marriage we were always together. I worked for him—that's how I met him. Our job situations diversified, but then I came back and worked for him again. So we were always, always together."

The Silvers feel their family theme incorporates communication. The importance of interacting is apparent. Like the Stouffers, the Silvers share the talk time during the interview. While the Stouffers are egalitarian, the Silvers are competitive and assertive. The Stouffers present an orchestrated waltz in which both partners know the next step. The Silvers perform an awkward polka. They interrupt each other, overlap the other's comments, and disagree. Both wish to talk and compete to do so. Although their conversational moves are not smooth, this couple provides provocative information on the role of communication in long and happy marriages.

• • •

Do long-term happily married couples have pet names for each other or do they use other terms of endearment? Many do. Researchers have shown that couples often use "baby talk" or special verbal intimacies that define the relationship.

Peg and Art Adams are from Connecticut. She stands six inches taller than her husband and was a receptionist and telephone switchboard operator when she was younger. Art worked in the mills. The two have been married fifty-seven years; Art is eighty and Peg is seventy-six. The two are down to earth. Peg Adams is suspicious of people who call each other "Darling" and "Dear." She reports, "I see a lot of other marriages and you think they're ideal. When you're together with them, they're calling each other 'Dear' and 'Darling.' I say to Art, 'How come we don't do that? But then they don't get along. So I see it as a big sham."

Art discloses that even though Peg doesn't use endearments, he does. "I call her 'Sweetie,' 'Honey,' and 'Gussie.' " (Peg's middle name is Augusta, and this is his special name for her.)

Peg recalls, "We were in a drop-in center one time and somebody heard him call me 'Gussie' and they started calling me that. I told them to cut that out. I don't want anybody calling me that but him."

George and Jackie Stanowski use the term "Lovey" for each other and sign their greeting cards to each other with this term. This expression originated with George, who, when he was upset with Jackie, said, "Up your everlasting, Lovey." Although the phrase is clearly not complimentary, he continues to use the phrase in public as well as private. Jackie is not offended by his use of the words. She relates, "Everybody back home picked up on this, but I thought it was just normal."

The fun-loving Callahans use a number of pet names. Susie remembers, "Oh, he has many names for me. The first ten years we were married, he had a different name for me every week, and I don't know how he even thought them all up. I can't even remember them, but he always had crazy names for me. The one he used most often was 'Susie-Should-Have-Said.' He still uses that one."

Jim smiles as he acknowledges, "I still do that."

Susie reveals, "He called me 'Downs' all the time. He tucks me into bed. He had to get up before I did, and he would tuck me in again."

Does Susie like this treatment? "Oh, yeah, who wouldn't?"

Jim rehearses, "Hi, Downs! I'se goin' off to play golf. Bye Downs! I'se goin' off to make money. 'Nite, Downs!' "

Alexander and Peggy Smith, an egalitarian couple from Illinois, laugh when they are asked about special terms. Earlier in the interview the couple has shared some sobering information about their child who died as a little boy. Their spontaneous humor now demonstrates their genuine delight with the question. Peggy begins, "My middle name is Alice. Once in awhile . . ." She interrupts herself with a cackle.

Alex is laughing, too, but he helps out, "She doesn't like it a bit."

Laughing, Peggy continues, "He calls me that. He doesn't do it to make me angry, he does it to be funny. A few times, he has done it in front of people. He'd say something about Alice and (she laughs again) they would say, 'Who's that?' "

Alex concludes, "We had a one-room apartment when we were first married and we shared a bathroom with two other couples. One of these couples had a huge black mutt, and her name was Alice. (He laughs heartily.) When I say the name, all we can think of is this huge black dog with this lopsided smile plastered all over its face." (They both roar.)

The Ellisons, including the expansive Evelyn and the reserved Duncan, have special names, too. Evelyn begins, "When we first got married, he called me 'Honey' all the time. It's 'Honey this' and 'Honey that,' and when my daughter was born, rather than call me 'mother,' she called me 'Honey,' too. This went on a long time. They all called me 'Honey.' "

Evelyn is called by other names, too. Duncan recalls, "I always called her Lester [her middle name] because her mother did and my parents did, too."

Like the Stanowskis, they also used terms that sound offensive to others, but apparently are not to them. Evelyn laughed, "I did used to use one name for him. I won't tell you." With a little prompting, she offers, "He used to call me 'Shithead' and I'd call him 'Egghead.' "

Duncan quickly adds, "But 'Honey' was the first name I called her. That kind of got lost in the shuffle after a bit."

Some couples use animal terms or other endearments. Perhaps the most original was offered by the Rizzos. Joe smiles. "I call her my little manatee. 'Manatee' for the local fish in the Atlantic Ocean and the Gulf." This aquatic mammal is sometimes referred to as a sea cow, but I wasn't about to share my information with the Rizzos.

Marital satisfaction may be more highly related to the perceptions of, rather than the behavior of, disclosing. Some research suggests the amount of self-disclosure occurring between a couple may be irrelevant to the level of satisfaction expressed. Gottman, an important marital communication researcher, holds the importance of self-disclosure may be overrated. He avers, "Couples in nondistressed marriages are indirect; they mindread rather than directly ask about feelings."

A couple's perceptions of how much they share may be discrepant from the actual amount that does occur. Indeed, their perceptions may be more important than the amount of disclosure in which they engage. Four different studies show conclusively that individuals who are highly satisfied are more likely than those who held low levels of marital happiness to selectively distort the amount of information they shared. Happier couples believe they share more information than they actually do.

Intimacy is essential to happy long-term marriages. Sharing information, mind reading, and using special terms of endearment all mark the satisfied couple. At the same time, self-disclosure is not a one-dimensional trait which can be prescribed universally for marital satisfaction. More is not necessarily better. However, no one recommends the absence or minimization of self-disclosure among couples.

The cautions surrounding verbal intimacy should not encourage younger couples to avoid disclosure. While there may be some forces in our society today that do support such a notion, contemporary writers have been clear about the problems this would cause. Harold Kushner, in his book *When All You've Ever Wanted Isn't Enough: The Search for a Life that Matters*, writes,

> I am afraid that we may be raising a generation of young people who will grow up afraid to love, afraid to give themselves completely to another person, because they will have seen how much it hurts to take the risk of loving and have it not work out. . . So Simon and Garfunkel sang to the young people of the sixties, "If I never loved, I never would have cried. . . .I touch no one and no one touches me. . . . I am a rock, I am an island. . . and a rock feels no pain, and an island never cries."

Kushner shares the ideas of others as he adds,

> Psychologist Herbert Hendin has written of the fear of true intimacy in people growing up today. Serious involvement is a trap; it limits your options. Caring leaves you vulnerable to disappointment and rejection. Having children does not represent fulfillment and immortality, but obligation and inconvenience. He writes: "Twenty years ago, detachment and inability to feel pleasure were considered signs of schizophrenia. Today, people believe that emotional involvement invites disaster, and detachment offers the best means of survival." In our work, in our play, even in our sexual lives, we want to be like machines (we speak of being "turned on"), performing but not caring too deeply.

Couples engage in verbal sharing, as we have discussed in this chapter. They also participate in the physical sharing of themselves. Do couples in long-term marriages have active sex lives? Are septuagenarians sexless? Do couples replace their sexual behavior with other activities? The physical side of happily married couples, particularly those married for forty years or more, is bound to surprise you.

Chapter 8

Sexually Satisfied:"I Think I've Died and Gone to Heaven"

When I first found out how babies were born, I couldn't believe it! To think that my mother and father would do such a thing! . . . My father, maybe; but my mother—never.

—Sam Levinson

Hugh O'Brien is a happy, smiling, round-faced and round-bellied Irishman who sports a handlebar moustache that is carefully waxed. His complexion, like many of Irish descent, is ruddy. Although rosy cheeks may come from alcoholic indulgence, Hugh's surely are inherited.

While Hugh is a St. Bernard, his wife is a Mexican chihuahua. He is calm and relaxed while she is nervous and high strung. Her body is thin and reedy. Mary Carol moves constantly and is flighty. She seems almost bird-like as she hops from one activity to the next in her lunch-strewn kitchen and chirps partial answers to questions. The couple has been married forty-eight years and are each nearly seventy-three years old.

They have maintained a highly satisfying sex life. Mary Carol remarks, "We've got a very healthy sex life. Nothing crazy or strange. He calls me 'Missionary Mary.' We've had a very good sex life even though I had a hysterectomy. There's been some diminishment over time; I mean, I'm going to be seventy-three years old in October." She adds with a twinkle, "I used to think when I was thirty that they didn't do anything beyond thirty-five. Now I think it's eighty, or maybe ninety."

Her jovial Irish husband adds, "For many years, it was once a day, and then twice on Sunday. I am serious. But as we're getting older, especially since I retired, we have more opportunity, but less frequency." But he adds with a warm smile, "It's still very enjoyable. The actual physical pleasure, which is there, becomes less important than the togetherness and the closeness, the physical touching." This Catholic couple has only two children, but only because Mary Carol had several miscarriages. It is not for lack of trying.

• • •

A great deal of humor surrounds the sexuality of older people. George Burns shares one-liners that suggest that he is still sexually alive. He explains, "I love sex and it doesn't hurt me, even at my age." After a pause and a puff on his cigar, he adds, "I don't inhale." He quips, "Sex is difficult when you get older; did you ever try to whisper sweet nothings into a hearing aid?"

Bette Midler enjoys the role of Sophie Tucker in her concerts. She tells stories about the infamous woman and her lover, Ernie. For instance, Bette recalls, "After a wonderful bout of lovemaking, Ernie was very pleased with himself. He rolled over and said, 'That was my finest hour.' Sophie said, 'If that was your finest hour, you're fifty-eight minutes short.' "

A story popular to happily married older couples includes the dialogue between a sixty-year-old man and his new doctor.

Doctor:	For a man of sixty, you're in remarkable shape.
Man:	Did I say I was sixty? I am eighty-three.
Doctor:	Goodness, your father must have lived a long life.
Man:	Did I say my father was dead? He's eighty-one.
Doctor:	Good grief, man. How long did your grandfather live?
Man:	Did I say my grandfather was dead? He's 102 and getting married next month.
Doctor:	Why on earth would a 102-year-old man want to get married?
Man:	Did I say he *wanted* to get married?

Do the jokes about seniors and sex tell the whole story? Are they based on stereotypes or on actual practice? In general, sex may not be as important to older people as it is to their younger cohorts. Joe Volz and Joan Mitric report a 1989 public opinion poll which showed that fewer than half of older people think sex is important. About 35 percent of the women and 38 percent of the men think it is very important.

On the other hand, Janet Belsky, a New York psychologist, in her book *Here Tomorrow—Making the Most of Life after 50,* writes, "The 70s are far from a sexual death knell." Similarly, a study done at Duke University showed that 50 percent of men in their eighties had sexual feelings and 20 percent were having sexual intercourse. Finally, the National Institute on Aging insists in a paper entitled "Sexuality in Later Life" that most older people "are able to lead an active, satisfying sex life. With age, women do not ordinarily lose their physical capacity for orgasm, nor men their capacity for erection and ejaculation."

The sexual lives of older people may be a mystery because people do not often talk to them about this topic. The 1989 public opinion poll showed that while older people talk to each other about their sexual satisfaction and behaviors, they are uncomfortable talking to their own children about it. They may be accurately responding to their children's discomfort with such a discussion. Bernie Zilbergeld, a San Francisco sex therapist and author of *Male Sexuality,* noted, however, that most young people, especially the elder's children, are "shocked" if their older parents show any interest in sex.

Are older couples who are happily married discrepant from their peers in less satisfied marriages? People in happy marriages are satisfied with their sexual lives and most of their relationships include a physical dimension. Their sex lives vary in frequency, but sexual satisfaction is not dependent on high frequency. Researchers William R. Cupach, from Illinois State University, and Jamie Comstock, at Florida State University, found that married couples who are satisfied with their relationship are also satisfied with their communication about sexual matters and with their sexual behavior. In general, the better the couple gets along, the better their sex life.

Satisfaction with sexuality marks happy relationships, and Kurdek showed that couples who are satisfied do not expect sexual perfection. They similarly do not have preconceived notions about the frequency of coitus. Sexual activity varies among happily married couples. For some couples, sex is a three-letter word; for others, it is a paragraph.

A happily married man, Leo Salerno, explains. "I think sex is like an appetite. Sometimes you have a second helping and sometimes you may not. Sometimes you want dessert and sometimes you don't." This Italian husband speaks for himself and others in long happy marriages. Some of them indulge in second and third helpings and even go to buffet dessert tables, while others push themselves away from the table.

A woman with high self-esteem asks her partner, "What winks and screws like a tiger?" When he responds that he doesn't know, she winks and smiles knowingly. A number of the couples interviewed in this study might have told this joke. These couples view their sexual life as central to their happiness and enjoy an active and varied sex life. They defy the stereotype that old age and sex don't mix! The role of sexuality came up with the American Simonians when we were discussing how they spent their day. I ask them how they spend their evenings, and the sensual Cookie responds, "We have our dinner, and, truthfully, we have television, and then we have our sex life."

Cookie and Sam Simonian report a vigorous physical side to their relationship. They feel that sexuality is important and basic to a happy marriage. Cookie continues, "Sex is very important to my husband, and it's good that we're both at the age—he's seventy-nine and I'm seventy-two—we're still active. I think it's wonderful because if I wasn't and he was, then he is going to go out isn't he? We're very evenly matched."

Is the sex better or worse? Sam reveals, "I feel that I'm just as youthful as when I was a young man. My desire is the same; my body desires and my mind desires. Sometimes we tell friends about our feelings on this subject, and they think I'm pulling their leg. You tell them the exact truth about it, and they don't believe it. 'No way a man seventy-nine years old could be that good.' I say if you don't believe it, go ask my wife."

Fred and Harriet Davis are originally from Urbana, Illinois. Fred served as the police chief for many years in that central Illinois city. The Mormon couple has been married forty-six years and are in their late sixties. Is their sex life better than ever, worse than ever, or does it no longer exist? Fred responds quickly, "Better than ever!"

"It has probably decreased in frequency even though it's more satisfying," I conclude.

Fred is again quick to respond, "Oh, not less in frequency. No, no."

"So it's as frequent as ever and better than ever?" I ask, a little incredulous.

Harriet tries to teach a young dog some old tricks. "I think after you get older, you're more relaxed. You're thinking more of each other's feelings and needs."

Fred team teaches the lesson. "You're not worried about the kids running in; you're not worried about somebody knocking at the door."

Harriet adds, "Or getting pregnant," and laughs.

Fred smiles. "The inhibitions are gone. You're able to relax and enjoy one another's company."

Harriet has a postscript. "On Monday I went back to the doctor, because I had a hysterectomy six weeks ago, and the gynecologist right away said, 'Well, you can get back to your love life now.' I replied, 'Thanks, but you're about a week too late with your advice.'"

Ann Donahue, a Roman Catholic and the mother of seven children, agrees with Harriet. "I think our sex life is better than ever because we don't have to worry about pregnancy."

Bradley Martin admits that sex had been a taboo topic, but the couple continues to have a very satisfying sex life. He explains, "Sex was difficult to talk about. We were both rather staid people. And I think that was a rather tough subject. Then we had children and things just changed I guess."

"I suppose one change has been that your sex life has slowed down over the years?" I ask this eighty-seven-year-old man who has been married for over sixty-three years.

The general disagrees "Not a lot."

"So you have a very active sex life today?"

"Very definitely. Yes. We still love each other very, very much. I would say it's pretty active. I couldn't say it's once a week or once a day, 'cause we have sex whenever it's convenient."

"People sometimes hold the stereotype that their grandparents don't have a sex life. And of course that's baloney. . . ."

He interrupts, "It sure is baloney."

"Older people still enjoy intimacy," I conclude.

He agrees, "Yeah, I would say most of our friends that we know do. And they're open about it. Very open about it. Only in the last twenty years have people been open about it. Before that you didn't mention the word."

Jim and Susie Callahan, the Boston couple, refuse to be categorized, too. "Has your sex life tapered off?" I ask after they had described great satisfaction with their lovemaking.

Susie responds, "No, that's not accurate."

Jim speaks simultaneously and emphatically, "No!" He adds a little less forcefully, "It's at least the same in frequency."

Susie smiles, "It kills the stereotype. We make love all the time."

Jim, joking, asks, "In fact, what time is it right now?" After discussing their satisfaction with their physical relationship, they conclude, almost in unison, "It's better because we have more time for it."

The implicit message from many of these couples who reported an increase in the quantity or quality of their sex life suggests that they now have both the interest and time for sex. They do not have the problem faced by the Italian officials who insisted upon putting a clock in the leaning tower of Pisa—they reasoned, "What good is it if you have the inclination if you haven't got the time?"

* * *

Mary Carol O'Brien fell in love with Hugh at first sight, though Hugh was not as quick to fall in love with her. Their parents had arranged for Hugh to drive Mary Carol to the University of Massachusetts, which they both attended. Her father brought Mary Carol to Hugh's house for the two to meet. When she stepped outside his home, she told her father, "I just met the boy I'm going to marry." She was eighteen at the time.

Hugh was not so agreeable. When he met Mary Carol at his home, he was reluctant to drive her to college each day. He reports, "I didn't have in mind taking any woman." When he found out Mary Carol was majoring in chemistry, he reconsidered and finally agreed to be her driver. "She must be smart," he concluded.

Hugh and Mary Carol both went to the University of Massachusetts for one year and then Hugh transferred to Wooster Tech (now Wooster College). During his junior year, he got appendicitis. He was rushed to the hospital during final exams and felt pretty low. Mary Carol remembered him with a letter sympathizing with his situation. Hugh was impressed with her thoughtfulness. He decided, "This must be a quality girl."

• • •

The men in highly satisfied couples exhibited a high degree of sensitivity toward their wives. Leo Salerno is philosophical, "If you make sex a mandatory, obligatory thing that you have to do, you take away from it. I think it should be casual, warm, between two people as a way of expression. I wanted sex more, but if she wasn't responsive to it, I never pressed the issue. I figured that when she was ready, she was ready. If you press the issue, you make a situation that is bad, worse. We never had any real hang-ups on sex. We figured this way, it's there if you want it. If you don't want it and don't need it, don't worry about it."

He is realistic. "When you do it, do it right." He pauses. "I'd rather have one good one than three bad ones. I never saw a bad one, but you know what I mean. I would rather take the time to do it and make it memorable. Sex for the man is something more animalistic, while for the woman, it is something that she needed and it had to be loving and tender. I always predicated sex on what she felt."

Cookie Simonian expresses the same sentiment, "He's very considerate. If I'm not in the mood, he wouldn't touch me. No matter how much his urge was, he wouldn't touch me. He's been very, very considerate. My mother-in-law used to say that a star was born in the sky every seven years, and Sam was the star that was born. And my mother used to say they made a mold and threw the mold away, and that's Sam. Now that's the way he is."

Ruth Ann Silver, a highly verbal New Yorker, talks similarly about her husband. She begins tentatively, "I think I can say that we've always enjoyed sex together." She turns to ask Ari, "I can say that, can't I?" To me, she sums up, "He's a nice man, he's a loving partner, he's considerate. I think I'll keep him."

Rudy Bemke, an egalitarian husband from Wisconsin, observes, "And we're not demanding. I'm not demanding, and she's not demanding. And we look at sex like we look at a good meal. She's an excellent cook, and she makes a nice dinner. And we enjoy it about the same way." Perhaps the way to a man's heart is only partly through his stomach. A number of husbands compare their sex lives to culinary delights.

131

Happily married couples are considerate of each other. These comments are consistent with studies that show that when women and men see each other as more equal, they report higher sexual satisfaction. Equal partners have satisfying sex lives.

Although many of the couples defy the odds and report sex lives that are as good as or better than earlier years, the majority admit a gradual decline in their lovemaking. Edward M. Brecher and the editors of Consumer Reports Books, in *Love, Sex, and Aging,* note, "[*M*]ost of our women and men continue to enjoy life, and to enjoy sex, despite. . . health impairments."

They pose an important question, "What proportion of men and of women experience a decline in sexual function after the age of 50?" The answer is equally interesting,

> For men, the answer is: *all men.* What's more, for most men past 50, this is not a recent phenomenon. Most of them have been experiencing a progressive decline ever since sexual function peaked in their early twenties, or before. Most women, however, do not experience a peak in sexual function during their adolescent years or early twenties, and thus do not undergo a steady decline from then until old age.

They conclude, "Our two central findings can be stated with confidence. Male sexual function undergoes a gradual, steady decline from the fifties on. Female sexual function also undergoes a decline from the fifties on." Many couples observe this decline, including Peg and Art Adams, Alexander and Peggy Smith, and Duffy and Snookie Day, among others.

Leo Salerno is one of the first to admit, "Obviously when you first get married, it plays a bigger part and when you get older, it tapers off."

The Italian couple from New Jersey, Toni and Joe Rizzo, spent the first nine years of their marriage living in Toni's family home. This warm, sensual woman recalls, "Our sex life was very important in the first nine years. It was good at times, but in the back of my mind the relationship wasn't the way that I wanted it. After we moved out of my parents' house, it was very important and very good from then on."

"Have you experienced a kind of leveling off in sexual activity as you've gotten older?" I persist.

Toni yields, "Yes, yes. But very gradual."

The Irish cutups, the Delaneys and the Donahues, discuss their respective sex lives. The men offer their observations. Ed Delaney reports, "It's not as frequent as it used to be, but it's still there."

Tom Donahue adds, "It's adequate."

Ann Donahue, laughing, is realistic. "You can tell they're both on the road to seventy."

Laura Clausen, a Presbyterian who has been married forty-three years, has endured a radical mastectomy. Nonetheless, she and her youthful, tennis-playing husband still enjoy sex. She stipulates, "I would say that for two people our age, we still have a lot of sexual attraction. Especially for me after all this surgery. A lot of men—I mean you hear the women tell this—the husbands really turn against them. They don't ask for a divorce, but they're colder. I can't say that's true."

Walter agrees, "I don't think it's interfered at all with our love life. We still have an active sex life. It's as good now as it's ever been, but not as frequent."

Laura opines, "I would never say that sex is not appropriate for a person of a particular age. If I was eighty-five, I still wouldn't say that."

"We were talking about sex the other night with another couple," Walter shares, "and I was telling them about my dental school days and this friend who was married but living in the fraternity house with us. He was always telling us about his marriage and it was once-a-month Moski. So it's not only age, but it's an individual thing, I'm sure."

Ruth Ann Silver is characteristically frank. "Of course, sex is not as frequent now as it used to be because he's been sick for such a long time."

Ari asks, "How often a week is semiannually? Of course, Ruth Ann's libido has altered because of the medication she takes; she takes an awful lot of medication." Ruth Ann suffers from diabetes and high blood pressure and uses medication to control both. He laughs and adds, "But thank God, my neighbor's wife doesn't take all those pills."

Ruth Ann laughs heartily. "I've seen your neighbor's wife!"

Julia and Ben Neilsen are a little more serious. The family therapist shares that she and Ben have always enjoyed a good sex life. "I think we're much more loving now than in the first twenty years. I would say that was one of the glues that held us together. It is less frequent over time, but I'm very grateful that I knew that from my training. Because sometimes people get a little scared when they see the changes."

Ben adds, "One of the physiological changes for a couple as they get older is something they should talk about in terms of sexuality, that there are positions that are much more comfortable and less athletic. I think that's important because it doesn't have to be an athletic event. You can adapt very sweetly."

Julia agrees, "I think sex is much sweeter. When you're young you're vigorous and it isn't really a wham-bam, but it is a lot more wham-bam. I find it much sweeter."

Ben laughs, "Less like a rabbit and more like an elephant."

"I think you really take the time to pleasure each other," Julia postulates.

Ben says, "One of the things we have a lot of fun with now, not only between us, but also with our kids, is teasing them about the number of times they interrupted us when we were having intercourse. It happened with just about every one of them. We got a really good kick out of that."

Julia remembers, "Then the oldest one, just a year or two ago, she called and she said she was coming over. I said, 'Well, yeah, take your time.' She said she needed to get something. I said, 'Don't hurry, honey, don't hurry,' She came over and we weren't around. She came up the stairs and she knocked on our door and we ignored her. When we came down later, she said, 'I apologize. I apologize. All I could think about was that you had had a stroke or something had happened. I forgot you have an active sex life.' It was fun to be able to enjoy that with her. I said to her, 'How many times are you getting interrupted?' "

Julia tells about another incident. "I saw one of my friends and I said, 'How's retirement?' He said, 'Wonderful, we make love in the living room, the dining room.' This was some time ago and we weren't there yet, but now we are and it's one of the greatest pleasures. So that gives an added joy."

"Yeah, yeah," Ben agrees. "Five years ago we thought we should learn how to dance so we went to ballroom dance class, and God, I thought we'd die. We had to get out of there. It was awful. It should be nice, it should be good. Maybe someday we'll learn how to do that—get into a pattern and have it still flow. Right now I can't do it."

Julia thinks out loud. "We do square dancing and that's fun."
Ben allows, "That's patterned, but it has a beautiful flow."

"We love to dance, really, it's our second favorite physical activity," Julia concludes.

• • •

*Hugh and Mary Carol were married in 1943, during the Second
World War. Hugh was commissioned an ensign in the Navy the day of their
wedding. Why did they marry before Hugh left for the war? Mary Carol
explains, "I was in love with him. My father advised against it because he
said I would be left with a baby. I told him I loved him and how did I
know he was coming back? So I married him. I told him [her father] that I
would rather marry him for a day than not at all."*

*The two were married in Notre Dame, in Indiana, not France, on
March 30. On their first anniversary, their son was born. On his eighteenth
birthday, his parents' nineteenth anniversary, he was accepted to Notre
Dame. Just as Mary Carol's father predicted, she did become pregnant and
she was left with the baby when Hugh went off to the war. The couple later
had another son, completing their family; however, Mary Carol miscarried
an additional six times, for eight total pregnancies.*

*They were together for one year before Hugh was sent overseas by the
Navy. Two weeks later, their first child was born. Mary Carol bore the son
alone. The timing was particularly traumatic since her own father had died
the month before. She remembers, "That was a terrible time. That loneliness.
I had to bring up John alone. He [Hugh] didn't see him at all until he was
two years old."*

• • •

For a few older couples, sex becomes an historical artifact.
Wardell Pomeroy, the pioneering sexologist who served as Dr.
Alfred Kinsey's chief aid in writing the landmark human sexuality
books, claims that sex is "just as enjoyable for older persons, although they don't have sex as often." He adds that no senior
should be forced to have sex. It is not harmful to go without sex,
but neither is it harmful to enjoy a rich and varied sex life into
one's senior years. Some people in long-term marriages have physical limitations placed on their sexual abilities. Edward M. Brecher
and the editors of Consumer Reports Books explain.

Some women and men remain in excellent health into their eighties and perhaps beyond—but some do not. Some women and men remain sexually active, and maintain a high level of sexual enjoyment, into their eighties and perhaps beyond—but some do not. . . .We find that impaired health . . . has a measurably adverse impact on sexual function. The impact, however, is quite modest—smaller, for example, than the adverse impact of aging on sexual function. This is true both for impaired health in general and for the seven specific health factors for which we have sexual data: heart attack, diabetes, the taking of anti-hypertensive medication, hysterectomy, ovariectomy, mastectomy, and prostrate surgery.

Perhaps it was impaired health or aging that encouraged a member of the Texas state legislature to speak in favor of a bill to outlaw certain kinds of sexual behavior. The elder statesman argued, "There are three things wrong with this so-called New Morality. It violates the laws of God. It violates the laws of Texas. And I'm too old to take advantage of it."

Some of the long-term happily married couples concur that disease and medication have curtailed their sexual activity. The Dahlquists, New York restauranteurs, have both undergone bypass surgery, which terminated their sex life. Darlene remarks, "The surgery had a lot of effect on it."

Leonard agrees, "I would say so, yeah."

Darlene laments, "I miss it. We don't have a sex life and I miss it. It was Leonard's surgery, not mine, that curtailed it. I don't know how he feels, but what can you do?"

Leonard admits, "The bypass surgery really curtailed it. We were really active."

"And very happily. Very, very happily," Darlene notes.

"We were evenly matched. It really jinxed the whole thing—that bypass surgery."

The couple disclosed that they had never talked about the end of their sex life before the interview. Although their sex life is over, it is clear that their love life is not.

How do couples who have experienced a gradual diminishment or a complete cessation of sexual activity cope? Most of them compensate with other behaviors, including increased touch, physical closeness, hugging, kissing, and similar activities. A number of them talked about routinized kissing, hugging, and other forms of touch. Nancy Stouffer notes, "People have commented over the years that when we walk down the street, we hold hands. He never lets me get out of a car alone; he's always there to help me. He holds my hand when we walk across a street. Even in a store, we walk hand in hand or arm in arm." The couple does not mind the public display of affection.

The Stouffers enjoy another public custom each Sunday. Nancy explains, "Our church has the nice habit of saying 'Peace of Christ be with you' and we shake hands with each other. Don and I always kiss at that point and say, 'Peace to you, dear.' This means peace in our life."

The Salernos similarly express their intimacy in alternative ways. Courtney smiles, "I'm always kissing him. I give him hugs when he's shaving. I pat him on the bottom."

Leo agrees, "We do a lot of touching. In bed we sometimes lie in bed and just touch each other. Or, we'll be watching television and I'll rub her feet."

He details, "She's got a bad back from surgery, and she loves it when I lay next to her in bed to give her support. She thinks I'm warm and strong. Some mornings she will be tossing and turning. I'll know her back is bothering her. I'll just roll over and put my back up to hers. It won't be one or two minutes, and she'll be sound asleep.

"Another thing that makes us feel close is that we will go to church together. We'll go to church together and not speak a word. It's one or two hours on Sunday that's spent with very little verbal communication, but we're together. Even walking to church can be good. If it's a service that she enjoys and I enjoy, it seems like we come out of church just bubbling and we're ready for the rest of the day.

"We also like to walk together. We just stroll together on the beach. She loves it and I love it. We never get tired of it."

Ben and Julia Neilsen enjoy a warm and responsive sex life. They supplement their sex life with a great deal of touching. When asked how physically close they were, Ben answers, "She's got the softest skin in our family on her hands. Never mind on the rest of her. Oh, wow! I like to touch her. I like to hold hands."

Ari and Ruth Ann Silver, not surprisingly, are more daring. Ari begins, "We touch each other a lot. We're touchy people."

Ruth Ann adds, "We touch each other all over. After all these years of intimacy, there are no holds barred."

Ari goes on, "Also we're not shy about being undressed in front of each other. We constantly walk around naked. We swim naked all the time in the pool here. If we are so inclined, we have sex, particulary if we have a porno in the house. I bring porno movies home. Ruth Ann finds them boring and repetitive."

Ruth Ann adds, "There are only a certain number of things you can do."

Ari concludes the discussion when he reveals that he often uses the fast forward and reverse controls on the VCR when they view pornographic movies. I decline his invitation to see their collection of films.

Other couples continue to view each other as sexual beings long after the actual fires of sexual stirring have been extinguished. Late in the interview, Ruth Ann Silver inquired of her husband, "So tell me, Mr. Silver, why have you stayed married to me all these years?"

Ari responds, "Because you're hot. You're a sexy number."

"Do you really feel that way?" I ask, remembering his earlier comments about the infrequency of coitus.

"She's very uninhibited, which I think is important," he answers.

"That's what brought us together originally and it's still true. He's a very sexy man," Ruth Ann adds.

Not to allow his wife the last word, Ari repeats, "Semiannually."

• • •

Both Hugh and Mary Carol graduated from college, he in chemical engineering and she in chemistry. Mary Carol has done some teaching and some research during her marriage, although for most of the marriage she has been a housewife.

Before Hugh retired, he was an inventor for Milton Bradley and invented strategy and children's games. How did he go from chemical engineering to inventions? He was hired in the Milton Bradley lab to do chemical engineering, but he drifted into game and toy development. He remembers, "They were near us physically, and I enjoyed that more than formulating paints."

The couple have been married for forty-eight happy years. Today they are retired in Florida, and they enjoy a meaningful intimate life. Although their physical lovemaking has diminished from the seven or eight times per week they enjoyed in their earlier marriage, they continue to make love. They have also learned the closeness that comes from touch. Hugh explains that in the evening they sit on the couch together and watch television. He amplifies, "She's an early-to-bed-and-early-to-rise person. She will lie on the couch and put her head on a pillow on my lap. I will rub her back and off to sleep she'll go." Mary Carol remarks, "I think I've died and gone to heaven. It's wonderful." The love life of these two septuagenarians could not be better, and it may be envied by both those who are spectators and those who are participants in the game.

• • •

How important is physical intimacy in a long-lasting marriage? The Consumers Union study concluded,

> Among other factors (in addition to open communication) almost as important were satisfaction with frequency of marital sex and comfort in discussing sex with one's spouse. . . . Among our unhappily married wives, however, most consider the sexual side of their marriage to be of little importance. This is the most powerful predictor of marital unhappiness for wives in our study.

Similarly, Schwartz and Jackson, from their sample of over fifteen thousand married readers of *New Woman*, concluded that one of the three key elements to a model marriage is showing passion in private and affection in public. They observe, "Public affection makes an important statement to wives, and its absence may be a warning that a marriage is in trouble." Women in poor marriages disclose that they are starved for attention and affection. The researchers write, "When the affection gap begins, the sex gap isn't far behind. . . .sex is a barometer for how healthy a relationship is *in general.*"

The authors of an important model of family functioning, Epstein, Bishop, and Baldwin, observe,

> Both husbands and wives must personally find satisfaction within the sexual relationship and also feel that they can satisfy their partner sexually. . . . A reasonable level of sexual activity is generally required. It has been our experience that

in some instances, however, both partners may express satisfaction with little or no activity.

Relationships without a sexual element are not dysfunctional. As we have observed, older couples in satisfying relationships vary dramatically from those with active sex lives to those with no sexual activity. Happy couples are distinguished by their satisfaction with their sexuality, not by its frequency or even presence.

When couples are not sexually satisfied, their relationship may be troubled. For example, Helen Singer Kaplan, who directs the Human Sexuality Teaching Program at the New York Hospital-Cornell Medical Center, states that women most often lose interest in sex because of psychological reasons. She believes the women become ambivalent toward their partners and this is often at an unconscious level. She writes,

> This means that a woman has a 'love-hate' relationship with her husband. She is emotionally attached to him, but for some reason is angry with him at the same time.

She allows that both physiological factors, such as medication, and a partner's lack of sexual sensitivity may also diminish a woman's interest in sex. She concludes, "The key to sexual gratification is a good fit between your psychological and sexual needs and fantasies, and his."

Happy couples report satisfying sex lives. Those sex lives may vary from no coitus to an increase in frequency over the life span of the marriage. The sexual behavior of the couples is not nearly as important as the construction of those relationships that occur through the couple's day-to-day interactions. Agreement and adaptation, and even a little imagination, are essential.

Sex researchers Masters, Johnson, and Kolodny, at Indiana University, maintain that communication about sex between partners is essential to a satisfying sexual relationship. Current studies by communication researchers similarly show that through talk, couples teach each other about their sexual needs, preferences, fantasies, and desires.

Sandra Metts and William Cupach, both at Illinois State University, suggest that couples negotiate their sexual roles and create "scripts" for their sexual behavior. Each partner auditions for a variety of roles until a mutually agreeable script is developed.

These scripts are probably flexible in long-term happy marriages and new roles may emerge as older ones are retired. Individuals adjust to each other to create an agreed-upon sexual script which spans the decades.

The Talmud represents the collected wisdom of the rabbis of the first five centuries. The sacred book includes this warning, "In the world to come, each of us will be called to account for all the good things God put on earth which we refuse to enjoy." Satisfied couples heed the warning. They participate in loving physical intimacy and they are able to talk about it successfully.

While communicating about intimacy is essential, coping with conflict is important, too. Couples do not remain in tranquil waters throughout their marriage. How do they resolve these problems? What does coping with conflict mean? Read on for answers to these questions and more.

Chapter 9

Coping with Conflict: "We Don't Let Anger Last"

The last time married couples agree about anything is when they both say, "I do."

—B. Lansky, *Mother Murphy's Second Law:*
Love, Sex, Marriage, and Other Disasters

Don and Nancy Stouffer's beautiful home, next to the country club, is filled with memories. The walls are adorned with awards and plaques for Nancy's community involvement, including one in which she is pictured with Nancy Reagan, who gave her an award in Washington in 1988.

Both Don and Nancy are tall, slender, and good looking. Don's gray hair is beginning to bald and thin. He looks a little like Fred Astaire in his later days and moves as gracefully. He typically wears short-sleeved oxford cloth front-button shirts and light colored trousers. As do most men his age, Don wears glasses.

Nancy is not unlike her namesake, Nancy Reagan, although she is much taller. Her presentation is both stylish and proper. Nancy has blonde hair, light blue eyes, wears glasses and a noticeable, but not distracting, amount of makeup. She generally dresses in warm blues, browns, and deep reds. She often wears a scarf at her neck, which covers the sagging skin.

Nancy is an organized, take-charge person who immediately ushers you out to the swimming pool to talk. She reminds you that the couple has an appointment that will limit the amount of time you will have together. Although Don is soft spoken and slightly built, he is not simply ditto marks for his attractive and outgoing wife. Indeed, this couple strikes you as truly equal partners. They take turns speaking, just as they share housework, meal preparation, and other aspects of their life.

The couple has been married fifty-six years and are in their late seventies. As Nancy wisely explains, "We don't let anger last, but we do have disagreements on things."

· · ·

Are couples who engage in conflict unhappy? On the contrary, conflict is inevitable among couples. As one writer noted, "If everything is coming your way, you're probably going the wrong way or in the wrong lane." Conflict occurs because spouses do not always share the same meanings for the events in their life. They may interpret such events differently. Unique individuals may bring unique ideas to a marriage.

Carl and Patricia Gronbeck, a highly autonomous couple from Wisconsin, often disagree. Carl clarifies, "We are so often on both sides of an issue. I don't care if it's an election or an issue. I was very involved in politics, and Patricia would be on the other side. I have to expound, and explain my theories. A lot of these theories I really don't like to expound on. Some of it is a prejudiced point of view, and of course, I had to explain my prejudices. She would catch me up in it. Before I faced my public, so to speak, I had already reached my first critic. The worst part of it was that I hadn't won her over."

Patricia laughs, "Yeah, he's usually in the minority." The two are different in many ways. While Carl is conservative, Patricia is more liberal; he is Presbyterian and she is Catholic; he is quietly Norwegian, she is explosively Irish. Patricia adds, "We come from different backgrounds. I was an only child. My mother worked, and I was pretty self-sufficient. I was raised in a small town. Carl was one of four boys and was raised in a city. His older brother was six, and the next boy was four, he was two, and they had a baby when his dad died." The couple proves the axiom that opposites attract and that they may have a marriage that is long and strong. Different voices can sing in unison.

Conflict is viewed differently from couple to couple. Some married couples avoid conflict. Tranquility marks the home of the

Salernos, from Elyria, Ohio. The calm, serene picture they portray is confirmed by Courtney, "We do very little bickering. I hate bickering. I can't stand it. It makes me nervous, so we do very little. Some of our friends bicker, but when we're around, they don't. If they do, I'll leave. I don't like it. My parents didn't bicker. I didn't come from a home like that. It's the only thing that makes me nervous. We do very little of it. We have no reason to bicker."

Peg Adams, from Torrington, Connecticut, said she and her husband do not fight, either. She recalls one child in their neighborhood who would come and visit because of the relative peace and calm in the Adamses home. She said the child told her, "I have to come over here, because you people never argue." She explains that the neighbors were always arguing at their house.

For other couples, conflict is a common occurrence. Sometimes it is the wife who initiates the conflict. Hugh and Mary Carol O'Brien, Catholics who have renewed their wedding vows, are a traditional couple who believe that "the husband is the head of the household, and the wife is the heart," at least according to Mary Carol. Hugh tends to be more liberal than his wife. Mary Carol's conservative values are balanced against her temper. She admits that she is usually the aggressor in an argument. She states, "I've got that kind of temper. I'm Irish. He's Irish, too, but he's very calm. He's never really gotten mad at me. He's maybe gotten annoyed. I get mad over things, but then I calm down quickly."

How does Hugh handle Mary Carol? He reports, "I let her go so far, and then I tell her to shut up. She has to burn herself out."

Mary Carol thinks it is surprising that her own father warned Hugh about her temper. Hugh explains, "Before we were married, her father said, 'I must warn you, you're going to marry an awful crab.' She *is* a crab, but she's loving. She gets all upset over some unimportant thing, and she will go on and on. I don't mean at me, but anything." He is thoughtful for a moment, and then adds. "But she's very fair."

Laura Clausen was the youngest child in her original family, and she usually begins the arguments in the Clausen household. She, too, is Irish. Laura begins, "It's all one-sided because he never argues."

Walter, the oldest and most responsible child in his original family, agrees. "Typically, I would clam up, and maybe walk away or something."

Susie Callahan was the oldest child when she was growing up. She explains, "I do a slow burn sometimes, not with him so much, but with his mother or somebody like that. If someone says something nasty to me, I don't take it to heart right away. I think about it later, and then I feel bad. Then I'm Susie Should-Have-Said. But I can never think of anything mean to say. We can yell at each other during the day, just some little thing. We just yell at each other, but it doesn't last long, if it lasts five minutes.

"I can remember the first time I was mad at him. We were married a few years. I remember I was so mad at something. I don't even remember what it was. I have no idea what it was, but I was just furious. I just remember being furious. Ten minutes later, it was all over. It was totally over. I guess I have a hot temper, but it doesn't happen often. It doesn't last."

Sometimes it is the husband who initiates conflict. George Stanowski is a plain-speaking Polish man who began and ran a precast cement business. Both he and his wife, Jackie, identify him as the one with the temper. Jackie relates, "His outbursts are very embarrassing. We have neighbors close by, and everything is wide open here. Because of the years at the shop, the vibrators and the noise, he is slightly hard of hearing. He gets very vocal, and he doesn't think he is."

George asserts, "It bothers her. It doesn't bother me any."

Why does George become angry? He states that the primary cause of his anger is that Jackie tells him what to do. He explains, "I don't want to be told what to do. Jackie has a habit of saying, 'Put the glass in the sink.' [I say] 'I was going to put the stupid thing in there anyway.' It's usually something I'm going to do anyway, but not just that minute." One wonders if George is simply defending his behavior or if men and women experience time differently.

Fred Davis, rather than Harriet, is the one with the temper in his family. Fred was the oldest in his family; Harriet was the middle child. She explains, "He has no patience with children. Yesterday, three little children came into the house, and right out Fred shouted, 'You can't stand up on that sofa!' It wasn't as if they could hurt the sofa. They were rambunctious children, but he just has no patience with children."

The former police chief asserts, "We brought up ours, when I spoke to them, I want it done. Just that simple."

Harriet laments, "It upsets me when he doesn't have the patience—even with our grandchildren, he doesn't have the patience I wish he would have. He'd enjoy doing more with them now, but he's not that type of person."

Conflict may lead to the destruction of one marriage; it may be the manner by which problems are solved in another and is thus viewed as essential for the continuation of a satisfying marriage. Happy couples represent the range from a near absence of fighting to continuous bouts of verbal sparring.

The presence or absence of conflict does not mark the happy marriage; however, the way conflict is viewed does distinguish the satisfied spouses from those who are dissatisfied. The common sense view might be that happy couples rarely disagree. This is not true. Scanzoni, a marital researcher, has argued that effective conflict and conflict resolution lead to a more intense partnership. Happy couples more frequently experience "positive" conflict, while unhappy couples report conflict to be a frustrating experience.

Conflict may be used for good or ill. The way it is viewed may make the difference between a long and happy relationship and one that is dissatisfying or terminated. Conflict may be destructive to relationships. Conflict may cause couples to feel less than satisfied, and they may be more inclined to terminate the relationship. However, some people thrive on conflict; others use conflict constructively; and still others view conflict as a necessary evil.

Conflict is destructive when family members do not recognize the inevitability of it. Conflict is dangerous when it results in physical or verbal attacks. Physical aggression occurs in up to 70 percent of families in disputes between parents and children and up to 30 percent of the conflicts between husbands and wives. Physical violence and verbal aggression are detrimental to family relationships and lead to the conclusion that conflict is dangerous and to be avoided. Mary Ellin Barrett, in an article in *USA Weekend* in September 1989, identified regulating your rage as one of the factors leading to a long-lasting marriage.

Conflict becomes hurtful when family members view the conflict as personal as opposed to issue oriented. Susie Callahan, from Boston, understood this principle. She describes their arguments. "We just yell at each other, but we never say anything mean. We never say anything hurtful. I think that's important. We never call each other names and never use bad language or profanity."

Conflict is damaging when couples view communication as one sided rather than as a shared event. When we view communication as a unilateral behavior, we see communication originating in one person while the second person is dependent upon the first. When we view communication as a shared activity, we view both people as simultaneous senders and receivers of messages. The first view suggests one person is responsible for the successes and failures occurring in communication; the second view gives both individuals the responsibility for potential success and failure.

How we view communication is related to marital satisfaction and marital distress. Couples who blame each other have less marital happiness than those who do not engage in blame. When we attribute the responsibility for a conflict to one person, rather than sharing the load, marital happiness decreases.

Finally, conflict is destructive when it is not resolved. The behaviors of one partner or the other may prevent the conflict from being resolved. Researchers Wamboldt and Reiss observed that stubbornness, defensiveness, or withdrawal on the part of the husband was associated with less marital satisfaction. Such behaviors appear to disallow conflict resolution. The Daleys, from Minneapolis, understand the importance of resolution. Gina admits, "We get angry, but it goes over fast. We never hold a grudge. We talk about it. We never let it go unresolved."

Michael adds the words echoed by so many of the other couples, "You should never go to bed angry."

Bradley Martin similarly admits, "We have many arguments. I have never gone to bed mad at my wife. I always kiss her good night, and earlier I could've cut her throat. I was that mad. There were never any really knock-down, drag-out fights, but we'd get mad at each other. We both are strong characters. I get mad over little things, I guess, and she doesn't just back down. When she gets mad at something, I don't back down, so we can do some pretty good arguing. But we've never come to blows. As I say, I never went to bed at night that I didn't kiss my wife good night, even if I were madder than. . ." The general leaves his sentence unfinished.

Conflict need not be destructive, however. Conflict apparently has a driving or energizing force, which is not unlike the motivation created by our physical needs, such as hunger, thirst, and pain. Conflict may result in physical arousal, just as our physiological needs do. Thus, conflict may produce a sharpening of our faculties, more efficient learning, and increased motivation to act. Some attitudes and behaviors encourage the constructive use of conflict within the family setting.

Coping with conflict is a necessary, but not a sufficient, prerequisite of a happy relationship. Other ingredients are important, too. However, Lawrence Kurdek, from Wright State University, explains, "Marital quality is related to beliefs that disagreement can be constructive." People who seek long and satisfying marriages need to learn how to deal with conflict constructively.

People who view conflict constructively understand that conflict is inevitable in human communication. The Clausens recognize the inevitability of conflict. Laura explains, "When you have two individual personalities, and you say you never have a disagreement, what's wrong with that relationship? I think lots of times after a disagreement or a conflict, the relationship is stronger. Going through a stressful situation in your lifetime, it either breaks down and you don't have any relationship or it's stronger. I think the same thing if you have a disagreement. They say that it isn't even healthy for children to be raised where there's no conflict. I mean you don't want conflict all the time, but they need to see how you resolve conflict."

Conflict is probably not only inevitable, it may be critical to the human condition. Writer Harold Kushner observes, "To be alive is to feel pain, and to hide from pain is to make yourself less alive." Later he adds, "If we believe that in order for life to be good, we have to avoid pain, the danger is that we will become so good at not feeling pain that we will learn not to feel anything— not joy, not love, not hope, not awe. We will become emotionally anesthetized."

Second, conflict is more constructive when it is issue oriented rather than person oriented. When the source of conflict moves from the person to the issue, people can disagree without damaging the other individual. Haim Ginott popularized this notion as he wrote in the 1960s and 1970s about parent-child interactions. He urged parents to let their children know that they were upset with behaviors and circumstances, but not the child himself or herself. For instance, he humorously stated when a small child spilled indelible ink on a new carpet, we should insure the child "we are mad at the ink and not at him or her." Ginott observes, "People are not for hurting. People are for respecting."

Third, the responsibility for the conflict moves from one individual to the interactions between or among the family members. People in satisfying relationships share the responsibility for conflict. They define conflict as something that occurs between them, not as a function of one person or the other. People in unhappy marriages blame their partners for their own negative feelings, and they expect the partners to change their behavior to minimize conflict. They also refuse or are reluctant to accept any of the responsibilities for the conflict, and they therefore see no reason to alter their own behavior. Robert Lauer, social psychologist, found that long-married couples were experts in the art of arguing gracefully. He observed that they approach conflict by saying *we* have a problem rather than *you* have a problem."

Fourth, constructive conflict is viewed within a cycle of conflict leading to conflict resolution. Satisfied couples hold idealistic attitudes about the probability of relationship conflicts and are confident of their successful resolution. The constructive use of conflict requires it be resolved, with a mutual respect for its occurrence and, more important, for the individuals engaged in the disagreement.

• • •

Although Don and Nancy Stouffer attended the same high school, he was not aware of her. Since Don was a year ahead of Nancy, she had heard of him and knew who he was. She notes, "We weren't in the same grade, and boys didn't look on younger girls." She adds wisely, "Younger girls might be looking on older boys." They met on a blind date when Nancy was a senior in high school, after Don had graduated.

Was it love at first sight? Don understates, "Well, she impressed me very much, and I didn't look any further." Why was Don attracted to Nancy? He explains that she had many qualities, but among those that were important: "She was very careful of her clothing. She was nice to be around, enjoyable." After fifty-six years of marriage, he maintains the same things that attracted him initially to Nancy continue to maintain his interest. He adds, "She's very tolerant."

Nancy Stouffer was the youngest child in her original family, and she admits, "We do have disagreements on things." She laughs, "I'm Irish. I flare up. I get provoked." She adds, "But I don't get provoked at him as much as I do other things. Conditions or something that happens will upset me. I also have a philosophy. I try not to worry about the things I can't do anything about. Only about the things that I can do something about will I give concern to." The Stouffers appear to have adopted a philosophy that we might all strive to attain.

• • •

Conflict is inevitable in human relationships and occurs in happy marriages just as it does in unhappy ones. Conflict resolution takes a variety of forms in both happy and unhappy marriages. Popular bromides insist that "talking it out" is preferred, but some couples use other methods to solve their problems. While they do not resolve conflicts in the same ways, couples who resolve their conflicts report high marital satisfaction. Couples who aspire to happy marriages may take comfort that even "pouting," "sulking," "shouting," and "showing a temper" are mentioned by satisfied couples.

Five common patterns of resolving conflict are denial, suppression, authority, compromise, and collaboration. When couples withdraw from the conflict and do not acknowledge a problem exists, they are engaged in denial. Denied problems do not evaporate, however. Family theorist Sven Wahlroos explains, "To leave a significant problem or concern undiscussed is similar to leaving a festering infection untreated. The problem will not go away; on the contrary, like a spreading infection, it will get worse." The cause of the conflict remains, and members may feel increasingly uncomfortable. The problem may become unmanageable.

Smoothing over the problem and minimizing differences occur when people practice suppression as a conflict-resolution technique. When they are engaged in denial, they do not acknowledge a problem exists; when they are involved in suppression, they know a problem exists but they choose to minimize it.

Women may be more likely to engage in suppression than men. Gladys Kennedy, a Methodist woman born in New Paris, Pennsylvania, felt that she was the one of the couple who usually began the arguments, but that she sometimes suppressed her anger. She admits, "I'm the talkative one. He's a little more shy. There are times when he's a little annoyed, I can tell this, and I don't press it. I'm not really a fighter. I don't like to argue." She and her husband have been happily married for fifty years.

Molly Frost is the oldest among her siblings and her husband, David, is an only child. This Catholic couple has lived most of their forty-four years of married life in Dayton, Ohio. Molly reports that she frequently withdrew from arguments. "It ends with my pouting because if I go any further, I'll cry. I'd rather pout than cry. I don't talk. He doesn't know why I don't talk. I don't leave the room. I do what I'm doing, and I don't talk to him until I've gotten over my feeling bad. In an hour, maybe, or even longer—I think I should pout longer than that—he's all happy, and everything's fine and dandy, and I don't like that. He should wonder why I've been pouting." She laughs at herself and continues, "He'll say something stupid or something funny, and then we're both laughing."

David adds, "I usually tell her I'm sorry even if I'm not."

Molly agrees, "Even if he doesn't know what he's sorry for."

"That happens sometimes," David acknowledges. "Then we kiss and make up."

Harriet Davis attempts to suppress the argument by sulking, too. She explains, "I sulk. I get real quiet. I go off by myself. I try to ignore him, I guess. I realize there's not a lot I can do about it so I just suffer. I think it just sort of phases out. I don't think we really ever deal with it or talk about it."

Fred senses a change since retirement. "Oh, I think in the last ten years since I've been retired, I'm a lot more apt to tell her that I'm sorry that I said something or did something to offend her than I was before. Maybe I didn't feel like I offended her when I raised my voice. But I know now that I have." He laughs as he acknowledges this new information. He adds, "I've mellowed a lot in the last ten years, yes."

A few husbands also use sulking or pouting to suppress arguments. For instance, although Nancy has a "hot Irish temper," Don Stouffer deals with conflict differently. He allows, "I pout a little bit." When does his pouting end? He explains, "I just need a little quiet time."

Individuals who routinely rely on suppression may feel that people should not argue, fight, or engage in conflict. They may misunderstand or simply choose not to attend to the positive aspects of conflict and conflict resolution. Sometimes people engage in suppression because they feel the relationship is more important than a seemingly trivial difference. Although suppression may be appropriate under such circumstances, some people routinely rely on suppression in all potential conflict situations. The reliance on suppression to resolve conflicts is not appropriate, although it may result in increased family satisfaction. Sven Wahlroos discusses suppression:

> Accommodating to the other person's wishes may be courteous and nice and lead to smoothness in living and to "getting along." But to accommodate or acquiesce when important issues are at stake, or when you yourself feel strongly against the other person's position, can be costly and dangerous. It can be costly because the price of accommodation is often chronic inner resentment and a feeling of being a "second class citizen." It can be dangerous because the bottled-up resentment may take pathological forms of expression.

When people use the power vested in their position, they are relying on authority as a conflict-resolution technique. The father in a family might act as an authority. General Martin remembers when his own father served as an authority figure to resolve a conflict between him and his wife. As a result of the incident, his wife became more of an authority figure on financial decisions throughout their marriage. He shares a story from his early marriage: "When I was at Yale, a number of the men had bearskin coats. Nothing would do but I had to buy a bearskin coat. Barbara just put her foot down, and said, 'You're not going to spend what little money we have on a bearskin coat.' I said, 'I'm going to.' "

"My mother and father were visiting us at the time. It was around Christmas time. My father took me aside and said, 'You know young man, you better pay attention to what your wife is saying, here. You don't have a lot of money, and you don't need a bearskin coat. You better just wear the coat you've got now and forget it.' I took a lot of that to heart. From then on when I got fired up over something and Barbara would say, 'Now just a minute, we don't need that or we can do without,' I thought twice before I said, 'We're going to do it.' "

Bradley contemplates, "I was surprised by Barbara because she was an only child and had everything she wanted, including her own car while I had to use the family's car. I was sort of shocked when she would say, 'No, we don't need that. Think twice before you say you're going to have to have it.' So she was much more the leveling and controlling hand."

Compromise occurs when spouses state their opinion and then some middle ground is determined. If you were eavesdropping on the Silvers, you would conclude they argue continually. However, they do not view their communicative behavior that way. This pugnacious pair had each been raised as only children. How often do they feel they have an argument? Ari's answer is surprising. "Well, weekly, I would say, we have differences. About house furnishings—I disagree with her."

Ruth Ann adds, "We fight bitterly about anything we buy. It's a conflict. I want. No, I want. No, I want."

Ari shares, "Most men don't care, but I have very definite ideas about what I like. So does she. So we disagree about that. It runs into arguments that could last for months."

Ruth Ann corrects, "Yes, but we resolve it. We compromise."

Like the other methods of conflict resolution, compromise can be used for good or ill. If people know they are going to use compromise, they might state highly inflated opinions at first. For instance, if a couple decides they are going out for dinner, one member might cite a five-star restaurant as her choice in order to compromise on a more moderately priced café that she really prefers. Sometimes the compromise does not embody the desires of anyone. A few couples named compromise as the hallmark of their conflict resolution.

• • •

Don Stouffer was the second youngest child in his original family; Nancy was the youngest. Both born in Toledo, Ohio, they completed their respective high school educations in the Toledo area. The couple moved throughout the Midwest during their marriage, and they have had a total of thirteen different homes in fifty-six years. They are Catholics who attend church more than once a week. Nancy is active in the church and serves as a reader in her local congregation. The couple has three children—two girls and a boy. Their son has nine children of his own, one daughter has five children, and the other has one child. They also have great grandchildren.

This couple spends a great deal of time together. They estimate that they may spend two to three hours apart each day. They do all of their shopping together. Don was in the meat business and Nancy calls him her buyer. They swim, sun, and walk together every day. Until Nancy developed problems with her knee and the country club raised their prices, the two had a golf membership in the country club and played golf every day. They participate today in the country club, but maintain only a social membership.

Both Nancy and Don have had health problems, although they look very healthy. Nancy has had several cancer surgeries, beginning when she was only thirty-five years of age. Two years ago, Don had heart surgery and has taken heart medicine since that time. As a consequence of the medication, he is impotent. When asked about their intimate life, Don replies, "Well, we're not dead yet." He adds, "But our sex life got terminated because of the heart medicine after my heart surgery." Both Don and Nancy accept this graciously, just as they accept not being able to golf together because of Nancy's knee problem. Indeed, the many physical problems of the couple are incorporated into their behavior with little fuss.

The couple is active in civic and community affairs. Nancy is the mover and shaker and Don is her avid supporter. They helped initiate a youth center, a park, and a beautification program in their community. Nancy has served as the chair of the beautification committee for three years. Their own yard evidences their interest in gardening and flower raising. These activities may serve as one of their conflict-reducing techniques.

This couple views themselves as helpful to family and friends. Nancy views their family theme as "The Stouffers are always willing to help—it's fun to be a volunteer." Don expresses a similar idea, "Take responsibility for each other." Nancy's family image is two rings entwined and observes "There is strength in unity." Don views them as a balance beam with him on one side and Nancy on the other.

• • •

The key to collaboration is communication. Each person recognizes the abilities and expertise of the others. The emphasis is on the problem, rather than on defending one's individual position. The couple acts as though a mutual decision is better than that of either individual. This orientation leads to a supportive climate in which each member can voice his or her opinion without threat.

Most successful couples believe in facing their disagreements and dealing with their conflicts. The Salernos, a Catholic couple married forty-seven years, typically use collaboration to solve their problems. Leo explains, "If you have something to say, and you don't say it, and you take it to bed with you, you're much worse off. When you have something to deal with, you have to resolve it. We're both pretty open-minded, and maybe she will prove me wrong, and I'll accept it, or maybe I will show her she hasn't seen it in the right perspective. In any event, when we're done, we both feel better about it. She's had a chance to say what she wanted to, and I had a chance to say what I wanted to. So we're not mistrusting anybody."

Mary Carol O'Brien was the oldest child in her original family and her spouse was a middle child. Throughout the interview, Mary Carol repeated that a priest had told her early in her marriage "Don't let the sun go down on your anger" and that the couple had always followed Father Collins' advice. She admits, "We never went to bed angry. He had reason not to speak to me many times." Not only does this couple not go to bed angry, they also make love each night. Hugh discloses that they make love once a day and twice on Sunday.

Peg Adams's Lutheran mother gave her the same advice to never go to bed angry. However, she reveals that she sometimes did, but that she could not sleep as a result. She reveals, "To this day, I still have a hard time sleeping." Peg was the oldest child in her original family; her husband was an only child. The two have been married fifty-seven years.

Susie Callahan adds, "We talk about it. We tried, at the beginning, if we had an argument about something worthwhile, to settle it, and not keep arguing about the same thing all the time."

Jim notes, "I can always get her out of it because she has a great sense of humor, and I can always say something to make her laugh."

Although collaboration may sound ideal, it, too, has inherent problems. If solutions to the conflict are offered as "either-or" statements, negotiation may break down. The couple's lack of time, money, understanding, or other resources can similarly negate the positive effects of collaboration.

Although the methods of conflict resolution presented can sometimes be exclusively identified within the family, most couples use a combination of techniques to resolve conflict. Former President Jimmy Carter, for example, explains that he and his wife, Rosalyn, solve problems by being direct sometimes and at other times by suppressing the situation, at least temporarily.

We have learned to address . . . disagreements more directly
instead of letting them fester. If direct conversation results
in repetitions of arguments, we have learned the beneficial

effects of backing off for awhile. A good solution, we have found, is for one of us to describe the problem in writing. It is surprising how ridiculous some of the arguments seem when set down in black and white, and it is much easier to make the small concessions that can end the disagreement.

But what is life if not adjustment—to different times, to our changing circumstances, to shifting health habits as we educate ourselves, and to each other? Jimmy Townsend says it well: "Marriage teaches you loyalty, forbearance, self-restraint, meekness, and a great many other things you wouldn't need if you had stayed single."

A variety of conflict-resolution techniques are used by satisfied couples. Some of them may seem less than helpful to the outside observer, but the couples learn what is best for them. Sometimes these behaviors change over the course of the marriage. Larry L. Constantine, a marital researcher on the faculty at the University of Connecticut, writes about his own marriage:

At one point in our young marriage, we had become aware of a pattern we seemed powerless to undo. Sometimes we would struggle for hours, and our problem-solving would escalate from discussion and debate to screaming anger. Somehow, we would eventually end up in the kitchen. I never quite understood why it was always the kitchen, but there we would be at opposite sides of the room, backs to the wall, voices hoarse and strained. Finally, we would just slide down the walls and slump to the floor in almost complete emotional and physical exhaustion. And then, a most extraordinary thing would happen. Last defenses finally beaten down, one or the other of us would say something in a gentle, near whisper, and that something was almost invariably what the struggle was really about. Worn down to where we could do nothing else, we would talk quietly and openly, and we would understand. Usually we would end up in the middle of the kitchen, holding each other and crying together.

It took us awhile to recognize this as a pattern in our relationship, and even longer to learn how to do things differently. Fortunately for our vocal cords, we did eventually learn how to skip over most of the first part of the struggle, getting much more quickly to the kitchen where we could slump down against opposite walls and get right to the good stuff of what was really going on between us.

Julia and Ben Neilsen have similarly changed for the better over time. Today they are more open with each other. Julia recalls, "In the past, I would keep it all inside."

Ben adds, "Me, too."

"I would be nasty, sarcastic," Julia says. "Again, that was my mother's pattern because she didn't know any better. Passive-aggressive."

Ben agrees, "We both were passive-aggressive."

"I think we speak up now," Julia says, "I don't think much goes by us. He'll say, 'You sound mad.' I'll say, 'Mad? Yeah, I guess I am.' I really think now we're in an awfully good spot."

Ben remembers, "We used to say, 'Mad? Who's mad?' "

"He couldn't stand it," Julia relates. "I remember the first time I lost my temper. I'll never forget it. Afterwards he came in and he said, 'There will be nothing like that in my family.' I was terrified. He would never hit me and wouldn't have even thought about it, but I had never been with anybody that was that angry. My parents never showed it in that way. That kept my temper down. I did it in a much worse way. It would have been much better if I expressed it, but dutifully, my husband didn't want me to do that."

Ben explains, "It was probably to show the outside world what a good marriage we had."

Julia is cynical. "We had the perfect family, didn't we?"

Ben remarks, "That's why I didn't want that kind of outburst. We wanted to show everybody how marvelous we are."

Julia clarifies: "I used to say, 'Ben you make me so damned mad!' I don't say that anymore. Now I say, 'I'm really upset about this. Do you understand where I am?' That makes it easier for him to handle."

The Neilsen children are bothered by their parents' new style of conflict resolution. Ben contends, "I think they're threatened."

Julia avers, "I think some of them are bothered by it. Some aren't—the oldest one is absolutely hysterical. She told her husband not to interrupt, but he did, and she stuffed a napkin in his mouth. It was precious. All four of us were in convulsions by then. Some of our kids are still in the passive-aggressive role, even though they're working on it, and they know they are. When they were growing up those were the patterns."

Ben admits, "We're looking at it as their problem. They've got to figure it out." The couple share a laugh.

Julia adds, "We don't worry about it. They say, 'Do you have to speak like that?' I say, 'Honey, I'm not mad. I'm not losing my temper, but I'm upset, and it needs to be out. Otherwise, I'm going to go to the icebox, and eat, and I'm not going to do that.'"

Does it bother the Neilsens that they parented their children as passive-aggressive people? Ben smiles, "Hell, if it hadn't been that, it would have been something else." They again laugh. He notes, "We keep telling our kids 'Relax—you're wrecking your kids, too.'"

Julia's conscience is clear. "I've made all my apologies, and some of them accept them more than others. I'll say, 'You know, I did the very best I knew how, and you're doing the very best you know how, and my parents did the very best they knew how.'"

Ben recalls, "I told my dad that one time. He said, 'Well how did we do?' I just answered him, 'Well, you did the best you could,' and I said it with all love and all respect. Why slam him? That doesn't mean you don't wish things had been different, and I'm sure our kids feel that, too."

"We're awfully proud of how our kids turned out," Julia concludes.

Couples who have been married a long time experience conflict just as do couples in shorter and less satisfying marriages. The difference between these couples and others may be the way they view and manage conflict. Happy couples acknowledge that conflict is inevitable, and they seek methods appropriate for them to resolve their differences. They use a wide range of resolution techniques.

In the last chapter we learned that long-term partners are generally satisfied with their sexuality. In this chapter we considered how conflict is resolved. In the next chapter, persistence is the focus. Older couples, like younger ones, experience many of the forces that tear marriages apart. How do they cope with these "slings and arrows" and avoid divorce?

159

Chapter 10

Persistence: "Being on the High Seas"

We continue to adjust to each other, but don't mistake it for a solid marriage. There is no such thing. Marriage is more like an airplane than a rock.

—Michael Grant

Leo and Courtney Salerno are an attractive couple who appear younger than their mid-sixties. Courtney notes, "We're young for our years. We don't act our ages, and I don't ever plan to." She is a full-figured woman, taller than her spouse. Her light blue eyes add color to a face that lights up with a fairly impish smile. Because she recently won an award for her dancing skills, she shows me pictures of herself festooned in a turban and wax fruit. While she might not draw looks from men on the street, her provocative dancing attracts a great deal of attention.

Leo is smaller than his wife, but has a profile that could have been struck on a Roman coin. His body is compact, strong, and muscular, evidencing years of athletic activities. Curly salt and pepper hair covers his arms and peeks from his V-necked shirt. His soft, brown eyes are among his most noticeable features. Women who are far younger than Leo notice him on the street. Leo exudes sexuality and a manly presence. At the same time, he is warm and inviting.

Leo Salerno, "100 percent Italian" as he notes, is a man of great verbal descriptiveness. He observes that the image of his family life with Courtney is "a flower" that "seeds, grows, blooms to maturity, to beauty, and dies gracefully."

He also likens their married life to the process of painting a picture. He observes, "I think marriage is like painting a picture. First of all, you've got to go out and you've got to get a subject. So you choose your spouse. You've got to pick someone up. Obviously, if you don't want to paint it, you don't pick them up. If you want to do a seascape, you get a seascape; if you want to do a still, get a still. If you're going to paint it, get something you enjoy painting. If you don't want to paint it, get another one.

"Then you've got to set goals. You want to go to college, you want to make more money, you want to be a doctor. Now you have to decide. You take out a piece of parchment. Are you going to paint on paper or are you going to paint on parchment? Now you've decided that.

"Then you have to decide. What status do you want in life? Do you want to be with the jet set, the country club set, the above average, the affluent? Are you going to paint in oil or water? You look at the picture before you start. What do you want to do? Do you want children? Some people do and some people don't. Do you want to be a success?

"Then, after you get all done, you sit back and you look at the picture. There's my life, I just did it. The picture stays and this is the mark you leave. That's why we're all put on earth—to leave a mark, to paint a picture. I think as we sit here today that she and I have a beautiful painting. Now all we have to do is put a frame around it. We're going to sit back and admire it." The Salernos celebrated their forty-seventh wedding anniversary in January 1991.

• • •

Happy couples are persistent. They have a sense of perseverance or tenacity about themselves. They refuse to let go of their marriage, to give up. They see their marriage as enduring. Researchers often refer to this characteristic as commitment, and they show that it has a strong relationship to marital happiness. For example, Clifford Swenson, from Purdue University, Ron Eskew, from the Hutchings Psychiatric Center, and Karen Kohlhep, from the Kennebec Valley Mental Health Center, studied the relationships among 210 retired married couples. They found that those couples who were committed to each other as persons had fewer marriage problems. Those individuals who were committed to the spouse, as a person, had significantly fewer problems making decisions and setting goals in their marriage, fewer conflicts over relatives, fewer disagreements about personal care, and less dissatisfaction with the expression of affection. Similarly, Stinnett and Sauer identified six characteristics of strong families. One was commitment to the family.

Although "persistence" is flatteringly called "commitment" by contemporary writers, it might more appropriately be called "stubbornness." Larry L. Constantine, editor of *Lifestyle* and a professor of family studies, explains the role of stubbornness in his own relatively young twenty-year marriage.

> There is a sense about our relationship, an unspoken underpinning of all we do together, which we sometimes think of as "givenness." It is not rational. We know fully well the hazards of modern marriages and the low odds of a lifetime together; yet, except for rare moments of particularly intense personal insecurity, we both seem to know we'll make it. It's a form of tenure; once you have it, you don't have to question whether your position as partner will still be secure next year. I feel like I have tenure with Joan. This does not mean we take our relationship for granted—dismissal is not unthinkable or impossible—but, short of felonious misconduct or moral turpitude, we aren't going to be sacked.
>
> Obviously, I don't have any inside track on the secrets of good relationships, but over the years the questions have helped me to focus on what seems to have worked for us. My marriage has certainly taught me a great deal, and I have come to look for certain things in friendships as well as marriage. Foremost, I have really come to value *stubbornness*. I respect it and even stubbornly demand it in my important relationships. Stubbornness is a quality which keeps people hanging in there when problems seem to defy solution, when logic or fear or pain might otherwise lead them to quit. The real value of stubbornness as I see it enables us to experience what it's like to get through things, to be on the other side and say, "Wow, look what we've been through. Bad as that was, we got through it."

Professionals in the human sciences prefer to talk about "commitment," which according to the popular rhetoric of this decade, is back in vogue. With many of us, of course, it was never "out." But commitment is a complex and abstract construct. Stubbornness, on the other hand, is something simple, elemental, even primitive. As such, I think it might be far more important and potentially more valuable. Certainly it has been for us. I think I'd much rather put my money on a relationship supported by a gut-knotting, perverse refusal to give up, by an irrational tenacity rooted in the most basic personal stubbornness, than on one supported by sophisticated talk of sincere commitment to mutual growth. The concept of commitment pales beside the adrenaline of real stubbornness when it comes to sustaining a vital relationship.

Stubbornness is the ultimate wellspring of history, and accumulated history is what has given us our sense of givenness. Today's problems look more manageable when seen in the perspective of some of the horrendous things that stubbornness has carried us through in the past. It helped a lot to be able to look back and know just when our marriage hit the absolute rock-bottom pits. In fact, when Joan and I were each asked separately what the worst time in our marriage was, we both named precisely the same moment of primal struggle midway across a storm-tossed lake in Maine. After that black pit of hell, we know we can get through the challenges we now face.

Many satisfied couples consider the fifty-fifty, give-and-take maxim and reject it. Walter Clausen, a former dentist from Austin, Minnesota, begins, "I think for a marriage to survive, the people involved just need to give more than 50 percent. You just can't get by if you don't. You have to give more than 50 percent in a marriage: it's just tough enough to make a go of it as it is." He adds quickly, "Even though I think ours has been easy—I think marriage is difficult."

Molly and David Frost, Catholics from Dayton, Ohio, and married forty-five years, agree. Molly notes, "You have to give a lot more than you take." David quantifies her thought. "I think marriage is a sixty-forty proposition." He considers, after a pause, "Seventy-thirty, I don't know. But everybody feels like they're giving seventy and getting thirty. It's part of the human condition.

If you go for sixty, and I think most of us do, then you know, you come out about fifty-fifty."

Mary Carol O'Brien, from Massachusetts, states, "You can give 100 percent of yourself to the other. Give 100 percent and don't keep looking at the other person and say, 'I did this,' and 'You did this.' Sometimes he gives 100 percent, and sometimes I give 100 percent. This fifty-fifty business doesn't work."

Some couples feel that anyone is capable of a long and happy relationship. Toni Rizzo explains, "You know my daughter said once to me, 'You know, Ma, the way you talk it sounds like almost any two people can make it.' I truly think that. I always tell my children 'If the passion of that first five or six months together was there at one time, you can get it back. If you let it go too long and too many hurts set in and fester, then you are never going to do it. You've got to be able to make the change before you hurt each other too much, because some hurts never heal.' "

Many satisfied spouses sound like the *Little Engine that Could*. Harriet Davis, married happily for forty-six years, offers, "Try to be patient. Things have a way of working out. It'll work itself out, if you really want it to. Desire is important. You have to believe 'You can do it, you can do it.' "

Laura Clausen observes, "We've had fun times and sad times."

Her spouse, Walter, interjects, "More fun times than sad times."

This wife, who had battled cancer and was battling it again, is firm. "I told you there isn't anything I'm going to let destroy me. That's the can-do attitude."

Why has the Callahan marriage lasted so long? Susie is small in stature, but big on insight. "We wanted it to work," she says. "We really worked at making it work. I think we had a super love affair. Everybody doesn't have that."

Molly Frost's response is similar. "I think we both wanted it to last."

Her husband, David, adds, "We had determination."

The loving Simonians concur. Cookie, a seventy-three year old who is as good in the bedroom as she is in the kitchen according to her lusty husband, states, "You have to work at it. You have to give and take."

Sam, seventy-nine years old and one of the most attractive and virile men of any age you may hope to meet, adds, "You have to have the commitment within yourself."

His American wife recalls, "My mother told me when I was married, 'Now you're married. You cannot expect to leave your husband and come home to stay with me. It's over. Your house is here, but your place is with your husband.' Every once in awhile, I'd feel lonesome and I'd take my babies and I'd take the streetcar all the way to my mother's house. Before I'd walk into that house, she'd say to me, 'Are you and Sam all right?' I'd say, 'Mom, perfect!' She'd say, 'All right, come in.' That's the way it was."

• • •

Leo and Courtney Salerno, the poet and the dancer, had an unexpected start. A wager prompted their meeting. They were both employed in a defense plant. Leo explains, "At work, I spotted her, and my boss had a case on her. He made the statement that he would like to get a date with that girl who worked in a certain department. I decided to get a look at this chick. There she was and I came back and I said to my boss, 'That's no problem.' He said, 'I'll bet you can't get a date with her.'

"We made a ten-dollar bet, which was a lot of money in those days. So I really started working on it. Finally, I made a date with her. My boss was really disappointed because he thought he had the inside track." Their relationship cannot be characterized as love at first sight. Leo notes, "We didn't date steady at first, off and on."

Courtney adds, "I was sort of stuck up. Being an only girl, my father always said to me, 'Honey, just mind your own business.' I was a supervisor because my father taught me so many things, and I would tell the people what to do, but I didn't look around too much. I was thought to be stuck up, and that's why his boss wanted a date with me. I wouldn't even give him the time of day because I was actually frightened."

Why did they get married? Leo explains, "I liked her personality. She was warm. She had a nice smile. She was always a happy-go-lucky person. I never saw her have a bad word; all the kids we ran around with liked her. Not that she was the belle of the ball, but they all liked being around her. She was a good time. She was a terrific dancer. Every time she came in, everyone lit up, 'Here comes Courtney.' "

Courtney decided she wanted to marry Leo before he wanted to marry her. She recalls, "He was a lot of fun. He was a devil. I had to quiet him down. We were both devils, but he was a devil in a different way. I was a good-time devil and he was a dare devil. He took terrible risks."

However, her attraction to Leo was more complicated. She reveals, "I felt in my heart that he needed me. He didn't have a mother. He never had the things that I had. I thought he needed a better life than he had. My mother was his mother because he didn't have a mother. [Leo's mother died when he was five years old, and his father served as the only parent to eight children.] It was hard for him and he needed a family's love, which he got at our house."

More playfully, she adds, "And I always liked Roman men. It was a physical attraction—his body, his looks—he didn't have any money. He was a very warm person. He was a sharp dresser."

• • •

Commitment in marriage sometimes shows itself in self-reliance. Patricia and Carl Gronbeck feel they have relied upon themselves. Carl Gronbeck, who had a career in insurance, recalls, "One of the prime moves was when I was forty and I had traveled with an insurance company for sixteen years and I had reached a point in my life that I just didn't want to do that. At that point, it became a family decision, not just mine, because everyone was affected. I explained to Patricia and she was very supportive. We went into business for ourselves. We bought an agency. It was the best decision that I ever made. It was risk taking. That's when the family gets close together." He continues, "These are difficult things for young people today to understand. You don't get the closeness by going out and buying a car together or buying a house together. It's when you jump over that hole in the ground, so to speak, and say, 'We made it, we made it together.' "

He adds, "The difference between the generation today and ours is that we had no backup. Patricia's parents weren't there, and my father died when I was two. We had no backup. There was no place to go. There was no running home to mother or there's no saying 'We're in a hole, we need some additional money.' The problem had to be resolved between ourselves." Nonetheless, the Gronbecks, like many modern families, have helped their children out throughout their adult lives. Their children have not learned about independence and may therefore have less-than-successful relationships.

• • •

The Salernos' home is restfully appointed in soft blues and greens. When you arrive at their home, you find them playing cards at the dining room table. The restfulness of their decorations and the shared activity serve to symbolize a great deal about this couple.

Leo Salerno is sixty-five and Courtney is sixty-seven. Both are Catholic and attend church each week, but counter to the stereotype, they are childless. From Elyria, Ohio, both graduated from high school. While she was primarily a housewife throughout their marriage, he served first as a highway patrol officer and then as a security person with Ford Motor Corporation. They moved only twice during their marriage and have lived in their more recent home for twenty-seven years. Because of illness, he was forced to retire at fifty-two years of age. The couple has a winter home in Florida and a summer home in Ohio.

The Salernos shop, swim, sun, walk, clean, prepare meals, have drinks, eat meals, and share coffee time with each other. They enjoy dancing, sex, cards, laughing, and travel. Although they spend the bulk of each day with each other, they have separate interests. He enjoys fishing, golfing, and spectator sports. She enjoys decorating their two homes and doing volunteer work.

The Salernos are childless, but they are regularly visited by the grown children of their friends. These younger adults see both Leo and Courtney as models for their own behavior. Neighbors' children frequently will disclose problems to the Salernos that they will not tell their own parents. Why? Courtney feels they are viewed as "a happy, understanding, and loving couple" by others. Leo explains that the two have always treated and cared for others as if they were part of their own family.

He describes their relationship with friends' children. "You know, we never had any children, but strangely enough all of our friends' kids look upon us as parents. Some of them even say they wish we were really their parents." The Salernos' style is reassuring, calm, and peaceful. It is no wonder that younger people are attracted to them as model parents.

• • •

Researcher Brubaker identifies partners in long-term relationships as "survivors." He notes that the long-termed married couple have survived the rigors and demands of an intimate social relationship. For many, the marital relationship changed over the years as they raised and launched their children. Then they moved into the retirement years and adjusted their life-styles accordingly. Their interactional patterns and communication strategies evolved over many years of intimacy.

One strategy used by people to survive in long and strong marriages is that they do not let other people get in the way of their happiness, including their children, their parents, their work associates, or their friends.

The Gronbecks tell a story that illustrates how a grown son nearly ruined their happy home. Their youngest son graduated from college. He did not find a job so he moved back home. The son began to change the couple's routine in the house. He would use all of the gas in the automobiles, but not fill the tanks. He would sit in his father's favorite chair. He turned the television set to programs he preferred, rather than to shows his parents routinely watched. But the straw that broke the camel's back was a banana drought.

When Carl came home from work, he had a ritual of relaxing and eating a banana. Night after night, he would return from work to find that all of the bananas were gone. He and Patricia would argue.

"Why didn't you buy any bananas today?"

"I did buy bananas."

"Why aren't there any in the kitchen?"

"I don't know—I put them on top of the refrigerator."

"I don't think it's too much to ask to have bananas in the house."

The Gronbecks recognized that their son's presence was destroying their happy home. One night, Carl returned from work with a new mid-sized automobile. He called his son out to the drive way. He explained, "This is your car that I bought for you today. On the front seat you will find maps to the major cities in the adjacent states. Tomorrow morning, you are going to get in this car and drive to those cities and try to find work. I will pay for all of your gas, your food, and your lodging until you get a job. You can take as long as you like to get a job, but you can't stay here. You're leaving tomorrow." Were bananas more important than the boy? No, but marital happiness was more important.

David Frost is asked what advice he would provide to a couple desiring a long and happy marriage. He begins, "I would start out by asking them a series of questions. How important is this person to you? They've gotta know that that person is the most important thing in their life. If it isn't, you better wait awhile until he or she is, or till you find somebody else.''

He remembers the night the Frost twins were born, and how he had almost lost his wife during labor. ''I thought about it a lot the night our twins were born. We didn't know that they were twins, and they were early. I was afraid of losing her. And at that point, that baby—and I thought it was only one—had very little importance to me. That's terrible 'cause I got two wonderful sons out of that. But that's the way I felt that night. She was more important than the babies. I thought about the Catholic religion and that I might have to make a choice in terms of the babies. I don't know, those thoughts went through my mind. If I had to make a choice, it's clear-cut.'' He turns to Molly. ''Did I ever tell you that?''

She is clearly moved. ''No, I don't think you did.''

Ann Donahue, Catholic wife from Chicago, considers the question of what she would ask someone who was going to get married to ensure they would have a happy marriage. She responds, ''Would you both put the two of you before any in-laws on either side?''

Her friend, Ed Delaney adds, ''Some mothers get so involved with children that they lose their husbands.''

His wife, Helen, agrees, ''Yes, that's true.''

Ann goes on, ''If you do put the relationship first, and your children see it, that makes for a better relationship. That makes you more binding.''

People in long-term happy marriages are also survivors in that they have lived long enough to remain a partner in a long-term relationship. Many marital relationships are shortened by the death of a spouse. Longevity is an obvious contributor to long-term relationships. As length of life increases, the possibility of achieving fifty or more years of marriage increases. In general, health seems very important in predicting life satisfaction, and it is probably an intervening variable in determining the status of a marriage.

Furthermore, as the length of one's marriage increases, the likelihood that it will last even longer increases. The National Center for Health Statistics provides the following figures:

Chances of Divorce

Length of Marriage	Rate of Divorce
1 year	50.9%
5 years	41.9%
10 years	30.0%
15-19 years	21.0%
20-24 years	13.8%
30-34 years	3.8%
40-44 years	0.9%
50-54 years	0.2%

• • •

Leo Salerno warns, "If they go into marriage solely for sex—you know, she's beautiful, she's a sexpot—that's not going to work. If she's going to marry the guy because his parents have got money, and she thinks she's going to fall into an easy life, that's not going to work. You can't buy marriage. You've got to work at it for a good long time to make it functional. You're going to have to sacrifice. If you don't want to sacrifice, don't go into it."

He concludes, "Marriage is like being on the high seas. You get on that boat, it's tranquil because you're in port and you're tied up. But you get out in the ocean and sometimes it gets choppy. Then it will level off. But the wind comes up, and the boat is rolling and rocking, and you can get seasick. There is no marriage that is going to be totally smooth."

Leo Salerno doesn't "rock the boat," either. He speaks fluently, eloquently, and often. Courtney adds supportive comments or side remarks from time to time, but Leo dominates the couple's talk time. However, he does not seem domineering. Courtney prefers that he speak for her. At the end of your talk with them, Leo observes, "I did most of the talking." Courtney quickly adds, "That's all right. I agree with you. If I didn't, I would say so."

• • •

Does commitment mean never saying divorce? Do happily married people ever consider or discuss leaving each other? Most say they do not, but some couples have considered divorce either in passing or as a serious alternative to problems and conflicts within their marriage.

Tom Donahue, from Chicago, explains that people married forty to seventy years ago did not think they had any options. When people married at that time, they married for life.

His wife, Ann, adds "We didn't consider any options. Murder, yes; divorce, no."

Tom jokes, "I used to tell Ann when she argued with me that she could go home and live with her mother. I was always afraid she'd bring her mother back. But I always said to her, 'Where are you going to get a better butcher?' We didn't have any other desires."

The Davises, from Urbana, Illinois, had also considered having her go home to mother. Harriet opens the conversation to say that they had kidded about divorce, but they had never talked about it seriously. Fred adds, "I say, 'Why don't you go home to mother?' But her mother's dead so she can't go home to mother. She can't go to my mother; she's dead, too." Did Fred really want her to leave? He answers immediately and without regret, "No."

Cookie Simonian, of Massachusetts, quickly answers the question about whether they had ever considered divorce. "Never, never. We have never regretted marrying each other. People have asked us, 'If you had your choice, would you marry the same mate again?' I would definitely say yes, and he would definitely say yes."

Have the Catholic Callahans ever talked of divorce? Jim responds quickly, "Never."

Susie adds, "Never."

Jim concludes, "It's not in my vocabulary."

The Benediks have never considered divorce, either. The couple is Catholic and have nine children. Wayne Benedik admits he notices other women. "Well, I've got eyes. I'm a looker, I'll look around. But I don't compare. I don't say, 'Hey, why don't you wear your hair like that girl?' or 'Why don't you dress like her?' She looks good the way she is; I'm not looking around."

General Martin has never considered divorce, but he, too, notices other women. I begin, "Have you ever thought about divorce? Have you ever said, 'This is it, we're going to quit.' "

Bradley looks surprised, "Oh come on, never."

"Not even kiddingly? You know how people talk."

He allows, "Well kiddingly, yes, but seriously, never." He continues, "Look, I've met a lot of women. I've never met a girl or a woman where I've had second thoughts like, 'Boy I'd rather have her than Barbara.' A lot of them I like very much. Some of them are friends. But never did I see one, if I just sat down a moment and gave it a couple of thoughts, would I have said I'd rather have her. The qualities that Barbara has are the best for me. Every quality she has are qualities I prefer." His comments are spoken like a general. His persistence is obvious.

The Nortons, both youngest children in their original families, resolved the divorce issue even before they were married. Their families worked together and sometimes got into spats. Herbert recalls, "One night we were at her parents, and my father and her brother had a problem. I said, 'Well we can always get a divorce if this doesn't work out.' Her answer was, 'That's not even a consideration!' And it hasn't been. In fact, our son and his cousin, both of whom have been divorced, told us one day that part of the problem that our kids have faced is that they feel they should live up to our marriage, and they feel that they can't. They think we're setting a bad example because we're so happy." The Lutheran couple has been married for forty-five years.

Not all happily married couples have been so clear about the impossibility of divorce. Laura Clausen not only thought about divorce, she once packed her bags. She relates, "Oh sure, once in awhile I'd say, 'You'd probably be better off without me.' "

She laughs nervously.

Walter clarifies, "Not divorce, but maybe separation. At least once she's packed her bags and had them sitting at the door."

Laura honestly inquires, "Why did I do that?"

Walter answers, "Because you were mad at me."

Laura looks puzzled. "I can't even remember now why I was mad, but I remember they sat there for a week. They were packed, too. They weren't empty. I think the only thing that kept me was the weather. It was wintertime in Minnesota, and I didn't think I wanted to get out and drive. That happened in the last ten years. The kids had already left home. I packed my bags one night, and I said 'I'm leaving. As soon as it gets light and the roads are good, I'm going.' "

Walter tries to remember the conflict. "It wasn't over tennis, I don't think."

Laura gives up. "I can't even remember."

"I can remember the bags being packed," Walter agrees, "but I can't remember why." These Presbyterians have been married for forty-three years.

For the Neilsens, the marriage changed when Julia went to graduate school and began to sense that Ben was "crowding" her. During that period, did it ever occur to her to get divorced?

She answers honestly, "Yeah, I realized that when I made the ultimatum. But I couldn't live like that. I don't know. I think I was prepared to go it alone, but it would have been extremely difficult. Five kids still at home, you know. I really can't say. Leaving, yeah, but I don't think the word *divorce* ever came up. We never actually discussed divorce."

Ben adds, "It was right there, though. But the way we weathered it [the change] is that we made the adaptation. We changed."

Julia goes on, "Some young people, when they get married, have the attitude 'Well, if it doesn't work out, we can always get divorced.' Now that kind of thought would never have entered, I don't think, either of our minds."

Ben relates, "She has a slogan on her wall, in her office where she practices family therapy, done in needlepoint: 'Divorce, never; murder, maybe.' "

Julia continues, "So I think that we probably put up with things. I think a lot of couples might just call it quits. It was just too hard. It wouldn't have occurred to us to get a divorce."

Ben notes, "Divorce never is correct, but it is interesting."

I ask, "What would it take to drive you away from each other right now? Can you have an affair?"

Ben's response is telling. "God, I would think it would be tough if she had AIDS. That's got to be just awful, just terrible." Rather than consider divorce, his first thought is the tragedy that could befall an unfaithful spouse through disease.

Relatively recently, the Ellisons, married forty-seven years, have considered divorce. As the oldest among her siblings in her original family, Evelyn was accustomed to being in charge. Although Duncan was the youngest in his original family, his masculine sex role encourages him to be the boss. Evelyn begins, "We decided we had to sell the house because it would be too hard if one of us died. I had a hard time convincing him because he was of the old school, the old family, where you had your home. I threatened divorce at that point, or at least separation. I said, 'Okay, if you want the house here, you take it, and I'll take the condo.' " Had the two ever considered divorce or separation other than that?

Evelyn seems almost eager. "Oh, yes, oh yes. Seriously, yes. You know, if you're honest, it's not easy. He was never jealous of me, but I was always jealous of him. If he would notice any other woman, then, oh boy."

I ask Duncan if he had ever threatened divorce or separation. He answers, "Not seriously. Well, maybe a couple of times." What precipitates his behavior? He shares, "She's quite an aggressive person. She likes to assert herself. When push comes to shove, she pushes too much. I think that's a lot of the cases. I just say enough is enough, and that's it. I can't spank her all over again and do the things her mother and father should have done. She would push too much. It's not just one way. It's not a one-way track."

Evelyn does not disagree with his description. "I'm inclined to be a perfectionist. I'm not what you would call a true perfectionist. If I can do it, they can do it."

"Living with a perfectionist is difficult," Duncan says. "I can't see it. I can see 90 percent or 95 percent, but that other 5 percent or 10 percent will kill you."

Evelyn is repentant, "I try not to do that."

Duncan admits, "I can't do it. I get to the point I say, 'That's close enough.' "

The Rizzos began their married life living with her parents and other family members. Toni was the second oldest child, while her husband was the youngest in his family. The period was stressful for Toni, who was home all day with her vociferous and quarrelsome family members. Furthermore, she loved to go dancing and socializing, while Joe was happy to sit at home night after night.

One evening she offered him an ultimatum—either they would begin a more active social life or she was leaving. She recalls, "Joe didn't say a thing. He walked out and sat in the car for a few hours. Finally he came back in and almost changed instantaneously. He started making plans to take me out to places. Up to that point, his family did not go out to a nightclub, to shows, or even out to dinner. They just did not spend money on things like that. Almost from that point on he just progressed into what I think made him much happier." This Catholic couple enjoys dancing, sports activities, and sex in their forty-ninth year of marriage.

• • •

A few days after the interview, Leo Salerno calls. He explains that he and Courtney have determined an equation that would describe a satisfying marriage. They offer,

1 person plus 1 person times 2 or more of love, health, happiness, companionship, and faith minus sorrow, illness, despair, divorce, and death. Multiply by the years of marriage. The higher your score, the more likely you are to attain Lasting Love.

A Conclusion

"It doesn't happen all at once," said the Skin Horse. "You become. It takes a long time. That's why it doesn't often happen to people who break easily, or have sharp edges, or who have to be carefully kept. Generally, by the time you are Real, most of your hair has been loved off, and your eyes drop out and you get loose in the joints and very shabby. But these things don't matter at all, because once you are Real you can't be ugly, except to people who don't understand."

—Margery Williams, *The Velveteen Rabbit*

Sources Cited

Acitelli, L. K. 1988. When spouses talk to each other about their relationship. *Journal of Social and Personal Relationships* 5: 185–99.

Alberts, J. K. 1989. A descriptive taxonomy of couples' complaint interactions. *The Southern Communication Journal* 54: 125–43.

Barrett, M. E. 1989. Still married after all these years. *USA Weekend.* Sept. 8–10, 18.

Baxter, L. A., and K. Dindia. 1990. Marital partners' perceptions of marital maintenance strategies. *Journal of Social and Personal Relationships* 7: 187–208.

Beavers, W. R. 1985. *Successful marriage: A family systems approach to couples therapy.* New York: W. W. Norton.

Belsky, J. 1989. *Here tomorrow: Making the most of life after 50.* Baltimore: Johns Hopkins University.

Bochner, A. P. 1976. Conceptual frontiers in the study of communication in families: An introduction to the literature. *Human Communication Research* 2: 381–97.

Brecher, E. M. 1984. *Love, sex, and aging.* Boston: Little, Brown and Company.

Brubaker, T. H. 1984. *Later life families.* Beverly Hills: Sage Publications.

Buscaglia, L. F. 1982. *Living, loving and learning.* New York: Holt, Rinehart, and Winston.

———. 1984. *Loving each other: The challenge of human relationships.* New York: Fawcett Columbine.

Cahn, D. D. 1990. Perceived understanding and interpersonal relationships. *Journal of Social and Personal Relationships* 7: 231–44.

Carter, J., and R. Carter. 1987. *Everything to gain: Making the most of the rest of your life.* New York: Random House.

Constantine, L. L. 1984. Editor's note. *Lifestyle* 7: 69–72.

Cosby, B. 1989. *Love and marriage.* New York: Doubleday.

Cupach, W. R., and J. Comstock. 1990. Satisfaction with sexual communication in marriage: Links to sexual satisfaction and dyadic adjustment. *Journal of Social and Personal Relationships* 7: 179–86.

Epstein, N. B., D. S. Bishop, and L. M. Baldwin. 1982. The McMaster model of family functioning. *Journal of Marriage and Family Counseling* 4:19–31.

Farrell, W. 1986. *Why men are the way they are.* New York: McGraw-Hill.

Fincham, F. D., and T. N. Bradbury. 1989. The impact of attributions in marriage: An individual difference analysis. *Journal of Social and Personal Relationships* 6: 69–85.

Fitzpatrick, M. A. 1977. A typological approach to communication in relationships. In *Communication Yearbook 1*, ed. B. Rubin, 263–75. New Brunswick, N.J.: Transaction Books.

Galvin, K. M., and B. J. Brommel. 1986. *Family communication: Cohesion and change.* 2d ed. Glenview, Ill.: Scott, Foresman.

Gilbert, S. G., and D. Horenstein. 1975. The communication of self-disclosure: Level versus valence. *Human Communication Research* 1:316–22.

Ginott, H. 1969. *Between parent and child.* New York: Macmillan.

Gottman, J. M. 1979. *Marital interaction: Experimental investigations.* New York: Academic Press.

———. 1982. Emotional responsiveness in marital conversations. *Journal of Communication* 32: 108–20.

Gottman, J. M., H. Markman, and C. Notarius. 1977. The topography of marital conflict: A sequential analysis of verbal and nonverbal behavior. *Journal of Marriage and the Family* 39: 461–77.

Gottman, J. M., and A. L. Porterfield. 1981. Communicative competence in nonverbal behavior of married couples. *Journal of Marriage and the Family* 43: 817–24.

Hendrick, C., and S. S. Hendrick. 1988. Lovers wear rose-colored glasses. *Journal of Social and Personal Relationships* 5: 161–83.

Hite, S. 1987. *Women and love: A cultural revolution in progress.* New York: Knopf.

Johnson, C. 1989. The committed nineties—Here we come! *New Woman,* Feb., 76–78, 80.

Jung, C. G. 1933. *Modern man in search of a soul.* New York: Harcourt, Brace, & Co.

Kaplan, H. S. 1986. I've stopped caring about sex. *Redbook,* Sept., 86.

Kelley, D. L. 1988. Privacy in marital relationships. *The Southern Speech Communication Journal* 53: 441–56.

Kirchler, E. 1988. Marital happiness and interaction in everyday surroundings: A time-sample diary approach for couples. *Journal of Social and Personal Relationships* 5: 375–82.

Krokoff, L. J., J. M. Gottman, and A. K. Roy. 1988. Blue-collar and white-collar marital interaction and communication orientation. *Journal of Social and Personal Relationships* 5: 201–21.

Kurdek, L. A. 1989. Relationship quality in gay and lesbian cohabiting couples: A one-year follow up study. *Journal of Social and Personal Relationships* 6: 39–59.

Kushner, H. 1986. *When all you've ever wanted isn't enough: The search for a life that matters.* New York: Summit Books.

Lane, C. and L. A. Stevens. 1987. *How to save your troubled marriage.* New York: St. Martin's Press.

Lansky, B. 1986. *Mother Murphy's second law: Love, sex, marriage, and other disasters.* New York: Simon & Schuster.

Lauer, J., and R. Lauer. 1985. Marriages made to last. *Psychology Today* 19(6): 22–26.

Lazarus, R. S., and A. DeLongis. 1983. Psychological stress and coping in aging. *American Psychologist* 38:245–54.

Lewis, R. A., and G. B. Spanier. 1979. Theorizing about the quality and stability of marriage. In *Contemporary theories about the family: Research-based theories,* eds. W. R. Burr, R. Hill, F. I. Nye, and I. L. Resiss, Vol. 1, 268–94. New York: Free Press.

MacKinnon, R. F., C. E. MacKinnon, and M. L. Franken. 1984. Family strengths in long-term marriages. *Lifestyles* 7: 115–26.

Manusov, V. 1990. An application of attribution principles to nonverbal behavior in romantic dyads. *Communication Monographs* 57: 104–18.

Masters, W. H., V. E. Johnson, and R. C. Kolodny. 1985. *Human sexuality.* 2d ed. Boston: Little, Brown and Company.

————. 1988. *Crisis: Heterosexual behavior in the age of AIDS.* New York: Grove Press.

Metts, S., and W. R. Cupach. 1990. The influence of relationship beliefs and problem-solving responses on satisfaction in romantic relationships. *Human Communication Research* 17:170–85.

Mutran, E. 1987. Family, social ties, and self-meaning in old age: The development of an affective identity. *Journal of Social and Personal Relationships* 4: 463–80.

National Center for Health Statistics. Reported in Barrett, M. E. 1989. Still married after all these years. *USA Weekend*, Sept. 8–10, 18.

O'Connor, D., interviewed by Donna Jackson. 1989. Finding the man you want. *New Woman*. Feb., 40.

Olson, D. H., H. I. McCubbin, and Associates. 1983. *Families: What makes them work.* Beverly Hills: Sage Publications.

Pearson, J. C. 1989. *Communication in the family: Seeking satisfaction in changing times.* New York: Harper & Row.

Phillips, G., and H. L. Goodall, Jr. 1983. *Loving and living: Improve your friendships and marriage.* Englewood Cliffs, N.J.: Prentice-Hall.

Pomeroy, W. In Volz, J. 1989. Good news for seniors: Sex lives on in later life. *Senior Spectrum*, Jan. 18, 1, 13.

Rubin, C., and J. Rubin. 1988. Tis the season to be fighting. *Psychology Today*, Dec., 36–39.

Russell, C., 1987. *100 predictions for the baby boom.* New York: Plenum Press.

Sarason, I. 1980. Life stress, self-preoccupation, and social supports. In *Stress and Anxiety*, ed. I. G. Sarason and C. D. Speilberger. Washington, D.C.: Hemisphere.

Satir, V. 1983. *Conjoint family therapy.* 3d ed. Palo Alto, Calif.: Science and Behavior Books.

Scanzoni, J. H. 1978. *Sex roles, women's work and marital conflict: A study of family change.* Lexington, Mass. Lexington Books.

————. 1980. Contemporary marriage types: A research note. *Journal of Family Issues* 1: 125–40.

Scanzoni, J. H., and M. Szinovacz. 1980. *Family decisionmaking: A developmental sex role model.* Newbury Park, Calif.: Sage.

Scarf, M. 1987. *Intimate partners: Patterns in love and marriage.* New York: Ballantine Books.

Schwartz, P., and D. Jackson. 1989. How to have a model marriage. *New Woman*, Feb., 66–68, 70, 72, 74.

Stinnett, N., and K. Sauer, 1977. Relationship characteristics of strong families. *Family Perspective* 11: 3–11.

Swenson, C. H., R. W. Eskew, and K. A. Kohlhep. 1984. Five factors in long-term marriages. *Lifestyles* 7: 94–106.

Terman, L. M. 1938. *Psychological factors in marital happiness.* New York: McGraw-Hill.

Thomas, E. J. 1977. *Marital communication and decision making.* New York: Free Press.

Turner, R. J., and J. C. Pearson. 1987. Through the years: Relational maintenance strategies of elderly married couples. Paper presented at the World Communication Association Convention, August.

USA's voices: Sharing, caring. 1987. *USA Today*, April 13, 4D.

Wahlroos, S. 1983. *Family Communication.* Rev. ed. New York: New American Library.

Walsh, F. 1982. Conceptualizations of normal family functioning. In *Normal family processes*, ed. F. Walsh, 169. New York: Guilford Press.

Wamboldt, F. S., and D. Reiss. 1989. Defining a family heritage and a new relationship identity: Two central tasks in the making of a marriage. *Family Processes* 28: 317–35.

Watzlawick, P., J. Beavin, and D. Jackson. 1967. *Pragmatics of human communication: A study of interactional patterns, pathologies, and paradoxes.* New York: Norton.

Zilbergeld, B. 1989. *Male sexuality.* New York: Bantam Books.